mytwocents

DR. STEVE EDGE

ISBN 978-1-64458-692-1 (paperback)
ISBN 978-1-64458-693-8 (digital)

Christian Faith Publishing, Inc.
832 Park Avenue
Meadville, PA 16335
www.christianfaithpublishing.com

Printed in the United States of America

For Diane

Contents

Section2: Reading through the Gospel of Matthew

SECTION 1

Transforming Your Prayer Life: Ephesians 3:14–21

Introduction:
A New Opportunity

Thank you for getting this book! This is a chance to reset, repriori-
tize, and rethink our lives. It is an opportunity to put the past behind
us and reach toward the future. I would like to challenge you in
two areas of your spiritual life: *prayer* and the *study* of the Bible. It
has been said that prayer is *talking* to God and studying the Bible is
listening to Him. I cannot think of two greater and more satisfying
areas of life than these. This book is designed to assist you in your
walk with God and with His Son Jesus Christ. Whether you have
been a believer for decades or you are just getting started in your
Christian life, this book will provide you with opportunities to grow
spiritually.

Section 1 is entitled, "Transforming Your Prayer Life." It is
based on a powerful prayer spoken by Paul in his letter to the church
at Ephesus. Here is a portion of that prayer:

> That He would grant you, according to the
> riches of His glory, to be strengthened with
> power through His Spirit in the inner man, so
> that Christ may dwell in your hearts through
> faith; and that you, being rooted and grounded
> in love, may be able to comprehend with all the
> saints what is the breadth and length and height
> and depth, and to know the love of Christ which
> surpasses knowledge, that you may be filled up to
> all the fullness of God. (Ephesians 3:16–19)

This prayer contains five petitions covering the following areas:

Living in the power of the Holy Spirit
Placing Christ on the throne of our hearts by faith
Being rooted and grounded in love
Intimately knowing the love of Christ
Living uncommon lives of abundance and fullness

Each day you will find a passage of scripture designed to assist you in a greater understanding of these five petitions. Here are my recommendations for getting the most from your study:

1. If possible, recruit a few others to walk through the study with you.
2. Personalize each passage of scripture by praying it directly to God.
3. Print out each passage of scripture and post it in a prominent place in your home (refrigerator, bathroom mirror, etc.)

Our Overarching Goals:

To experience the power of God as we give Him first priority in our lives!

To make prayer a priority and to experience the power of praying scripture!

To meditate on the truths found in the Bible, strengthening us in our daily lives!

May God richly bless you as you begin your journey!

Petition #1:
Praying For Spiritual Strength

Spiritual Strength

"That He would grant you, according to the riches of His glory, to be *strengthened* with power through His Spirit in the inner man" (Ephesians 3:16).

Today, we will be focusing on praying for spiritual strength. So often we speak of praying *God's* will. Well, praying scripture is a tremendous way on which to focus our prayer life because the truths found in the Bible are *always* God's will for our lives. In other words, praying scripture allows us to *acknowledge* God for who He is, *believe* Him for what He has promised, and *rejoice* in Him for His caring faithfulness over our lives.

So what better way to begin our study than to pray for strength—spiritual, supernatural strength that goes beyond our comprehension.

This strength comes directly from God, through *His* Spirit, and gives us *power*. This power gives us the ability to react to the world differently than those without God. Believers in Jesus are to worship in the Spirit (John 4:24), pray in the Spirit (Romans 8:26), and live life in the Spirit (Galatians 5:16). With God as our Father, Jesus as our Savior and Mediator, and the Spirit as our Helper, Christians can take on the issues of the day with confidence and assurance. Praying biblical truth is powerful and effective, so as you pray, be tenacious and be expectant of what God is going to do. If you are on the believing side of John 3:16, then Ephesians 3:16 is yours to claim and enjoy. Take some time right now and ask God to strengthen you with power, by His Spirit, within your heart and life.

New Strength

He gives *strength* to the weary, and to him who lacks might He increases power. Though youths grow weary and tired, and vigorous young men stumble badly, yet those who wait for the LORD will gain *new strength*; they will mount up with wings like eagles, they will run and not get tired, they will walk and not become weary. (Isaiah 40:29-31)

Today we see the magnificent promise of gaining *new* strength. The passage begins with a reminder that God gives strength to those who need it most—the weary. This weariness comes as no surprise to God because He created us and is thoroughly acquainted with our condition. He knows our frame and He is mindful that we are dust (Psalm 103:14). No one escapes the human condition and everyone is eventually in need of gaining *new* strength. And that is exactly what God does: He gives strength to the weary. Another word for *strength* is *vigor*. Vigor can be defined as being energetic and living with intensity. Are we living spiritually energetic lives? Are we living with intensity and a focus on Jesus? If we find ourselves weary and lacking these qualities, we can pray and ask God to grant us new strength.

The Bible also tells us that for those who are in lack of might (strength), God will increase their *power*. The word "power" can be defined as *staunchness*. Staunchness is the ability to be steadfast in your faith and to have a resolve in following Christ. But there is some criteria placed on receiving *new* strength. It is reserved for those who *wait* for the Lord. Waiting for the Lord literally means *being expectant* of Him. It is to have expectations that your prayers will be answered, that waiting for God *will* yield new strength in your life. Have you ever been involved in a physically demanding activity in which you began to feel tired? Then seemingly out of nowhere, your body adjusts to the situation and you get your "second wind." To gain a "second wind" literally means to obtain *energy* for a renewed effort to *continue* an undertaking. In this world, the Christian life can often be difficult and demanding. As believers, we can pray for this spiritual "second wind" at any time, but we must be expectant of the answer, *waiting* for the Lord. As a result, we will mount up with wings like eagles, we will run and not get tired, and we will walk and not become weary. We will have the supernatural energy to continue in the life that God has called us to live. Oh, and one last thing, we shouldn't be surprised if our *new* strength is greater than the energy in which we previously walked. God has a way of doing that!

The Benefits of Knowing God

> Bless the LORD, O my soul, and all that is within me, bless His holy name. Bless the LORD, O my soul, and forget none of His benefits; who pardons all your iniquities, who heals all your diseases; who redeems your life from the pit, who crowns you with lovingkindness and compassion; who satisfies your years with good things, so that your *youth is renewed* like the eagle. (Psalm 103:1–5)

There are benefits to knowing God and experiencing them is essential if we are to live a life of spiritual *strength* and renewal. Consider what God has done for us through the cross of Jesus:

1. God is willing to *forgive* us of every wrong we have ever and will ever commit in our lifetime.
2. God is willing to *heal* us from the things that prohibit us from living a victorious life (addiction, depression, fear, etc.).
3. God is willing to *redeem* our very souls from eternal condemnation and separation from Him.
4. God is willing to show us *love, kindness,* and *compassion.*
5. God is willing to *provide* us with everything we need to live a full and meaningful life.

I believe that receiving these benefits into our lives and remembering them daily acts as a way for God to *renew* our youth. Conversely, it is only when we *forget* what God has done for us that we become spiritually *weak* and in need of renewal. I believe that it is for this reason that the writer of the Psalm (David) reminds us to "Forget *none* of His (God's) benefits." So having established that *receiving* and *remembering* these benefits will bring spiritual renewal, consider the following:

God pardons all of your iniquities, *so that* your youth is renewed.
God heals all of your diseases, *so that* your youth is renewed.
God redeems your life from the pit, *so that* your youth is renewed.
God crowns you with love, kindness, and
compassion, *so that* your youth is renewed.
God satisfies your years with good things,
so that your youth is renewed.

So now, with a renewed vigor for what God has done for us, I believe it is now appropriate for each of us to proclaim, "Bless the Lord, O my soul, and all that is within me, bless His holy name." Continue to praise Him as you pray for spiritual strength today!

God's Power Toward You

> I pray that the eyes of your heart may be enlightened, so that you will know what is the hope of His calling, what are the riches of the glory of His inheritance in the saints, and what is the surpassing *greatness of His power toward us who believe.* (Ephesians 1:18–19a)

If you have been praying for spiritual strength, I wouldn't be surprised if you have had some distractions. Anytime God's people get serious about prayer and His Word, there will be obstacles. But don't let what is going on around you distract you from what God desires to do within you. Be persistent, pray, and expectantly wait for the Lord. Today's passage deals with the hope, the riches, and the power available to every born-again believer in Jesus.

Hope is a wonderful word and, although I shouldn't, I tend to stay away from it. This is primarily because of how it is misused in our culture. So often we hear, "I *hope* it doesn't rain today." "I *hope* my team wins the game." "I *hope* I get the job." In each instance the word *hope* comes with a sense of uncertainty. In fact, it *might* rain, our team *might* lose the game, we *might not* get the job. Hope is then relegated to mean something that the biblical term does not imply. Christian hope is *certainty*. It is "knowing" that something will happen even before seeing it come to fruition (Hebrews 11:1). It is not wishful thinking or "pie in the sky" theology rather it is *real* and it comes from a personal relationship with Jesus Christ. As believers, we should know the hope of Christ's calling on our lives.

Likewise, the word *riches* usually bring to mind material posses-sions; bank accounts, assets, investments, and so on. Yet the riches for the believer are not of the destructible nature rather the indestructi-ble. Material possessions are only for the seven, eight, or nine decades (on average) that we will live on this earth. *God's* riches follow us in this life *and* into eternity as well (Matthew 6:33). As believers, we get to enjoy the spiritual riches that are found in Jesus.

But in addition to this hope and these riches is the issue of *power*. Our passage is a prayer that the eyes of our heart would be *enlightened* so that we can to see the power of God that is *toward* us. It is a prayer that we would *experience* this power and *enjoy* it. "Eyes of the heart" is an expression referring to having spiritual eyes. This differs from how the world views things. Just like a blind man whose *physical* eyes do not work properly, there is also *spiritual* blindness in which the eyes of our heart are obstructed. When we pray this prayer, we are asking God to give us spiritual eyes to see the reality of who He is and to appreciate the hope, the riches, and the greatness of His *power* that He richly supplies believers. I hope you will spend the rest of your day expressing this prayer to God, enjoying favor with Him, and experiencing His power!

Petition #2:
Making Christ Our Priority
Through Faith

The Throne Of Your Heart

"So that Christ may dwell in your hearts *through faith*" (Ephesians 3:17a).

There is only one God, but He exists in three persons. He has a character and nature that never changes. God is who He is. In the prayer that we are studying, we can see these three persons of God. Consider each of these excerpts from Paul's prayer: "For this reason I bow my knees before the *Father*" (verse 14), "so that *Christ* may dwell in your hearts through faith" (verse 17), and "to be strengthened with power through His *Spirit* in the inner man" (verse 16). God resides in heaven with the risen Christ seated at His right hand, interceding for all who are saved, yet God's Spirit is also active on earth in the hearts and lives of those who believe. So how does *Christ* actually dwell in our hearts? The passage tells us that He dwells in our hearts *through* (our) faith. So how does our faith cause Jesus to dwell within us?

Two things we need to understand: the meaning of the word *heart* and what it means to exercise *faith*. The human heart resides in the center of a person's chest. It is the life giving, blood-pumping organ, without which none of us would be alive. When the Bible uses the word heart, it is not referring to the organ rather the heart's position (being in the center of the chest). Spiritually speaking our heart

19

is at the center of our *existence*. It is the seat of all of our thoughts, passions, desires, appetites, affections, purposes, and endeavors. It is who we really are and reveals the things that are most important to us. This idea is not foreign to our culture. Perhaps we have heard someone say, "I love you will all of my *heart*" or "He plays the game with *heart*" or "My *heart* goes out to you." In each instance, the idea of heart means *totality*. We can interpret each of these examples as meaning "loving someone *completely*", "playing a sport with *everything* that we have", and "sympathizing *wholly* with others." So the heart represents who we are and what we are really about.

So Christ is to be at the center of our existence and He dwells in that place through (our) *faith*. So what is faith? It is the conviction that God exists and that He is the Creator and Ruler of all things and that He is the provider of eternal salvation through Jesus Christ. In its most basic form, faith means to *trust* in God.

We can think of the spiritual heart as a throne and on that throne only one person can sit. Either we sit there or Christ does. As we trust God with our lives, exercising faith, we are inviting Him to sit on the throne of our hearts, which in turn has an effect on our desires, our appetites, our endeavors, and ultimately our purpose. God wants to guide us in this life and lead us to a much richer, rewarding life experience, but He must dwell on the throne of our heart and He does that as we exercise faith in Him. Today, why not vacate the throne of your heart and ask God to take center stage in your life as you fully trust in Him.

Seeking God

"And without *faith* it is impossible to please Him, for he who comes to God must *believe* that He is and that He is a rewarder of those who seek Him" (Hebrews 11:6).

To have faith is to believe and to believe is to have faith. Both of these words come from the same root word and both are descriptive of our relationship with God. Today's passage instructs us to believe two things: that God *is* and that He rewards those who *seek* Him. As believers, we do not just throw out prayers in the hope that, if God is out there somewhere, He will answer. We must *know* that God is there and that He cares for us. There is a passage in the Old Testament that I believe can assist us in understanding this concept. Consider the following:

> For I know the plans that I have for you,' declares the LORD, 'plans for welfare and not for calamity to give you a future and a hope. Then you will call upon Me and come and pray to Me, and I will listen to you. You will seek Me and find Me when you search for Me with all your heart. (Jeremiah 29:11–13)

I believe that the order of statements in this passage is extremely important for understanding God. First, God told Israel that He *had* plans, plans for good and not calamity, plans for a bright future, full of hope. Secondly, God said, "*Then* you will call upon Me, and I will listen to you." The occasion for prayer was *because* of God's plan to prosper them. Lastly, God told Israel that they would find Him *when* they sought Him with all of their heart. Seeking God would lead to knowing and understanding Him. All of this was done under the *old* covenant that God had made with Israel.

Compare that to what God has provided to us under the *new* covenant of Jesus Christ. First, God *has* a plan, and not just for Israel rather for the whole world. *"For God so loved the world that He gave His only Son… to be the propitiation for our sins"* (John 3:16, 1 John 4:10). Secondly, there is now no distinction between Jews (Israel) and Gentiles (the rest of the world) rather God will richly bless *all* who call on Him (Romans 10:12). *Everyone* who calls on His name will be saved (Romans 10:13). Lastly, Jesus tells us that everyone who *seeks* Him *will* find Him (Matthew 7:8) and that the one who *seeks* Him first, above all other things, *will* have every material need met as well (Matthew 6:33). Given these fundamental truths about God and what He offers us in Jesus Christ, it is no wonder that the writer of Hebrews says that without faith (trust) it is *impossible* to please Him. Faith is an appropriate response to a loving God. When we come to Him, we must believe that He *is* who He says He is and that He will reward those who seek Him. *Trust* in His love for you. *Trust* in His provision of salvation for you. *Trust* in His promises of richly blessing you as you call on Him. Seek Him today—the rewards are endless.

Salvation by Faith

> For God did not send the Son into the world
> to judge the world, but that the world might be
> saved through Him. He who *believes* in Him is not
> judged; he who *does not believe* has been judged
> already, *because he has not believed* in the name of
> the only begotten Son of God. (John 3:17–18)

First things first, why did God send Jesus into the world? God sent
Jesus to save the lost, the ungodly, sinners. The word "world" is used
three times in today's passage and it refers to *all* of the inhabitants of
the earth, the entire human race, the ungodly multitude, the whole
mass of mankind alienated from God. When you see this word think
of totality or entirety. There are three implications for the world
found in this passage: God loves us—all of us—God did *not* send
Jesus for the purpose of condemnation rather God sent Jesus in order
to *save* us.

Because of His love for us, God's purpose is not condemnation,
rather salvation. So what is required for someone to be saved? When
that question was asked of a leader in the first century church, the
answer given was "*believe* in Jesus" (Acts 16:31). Salvation is by *faith*.
So in what are we supposed to put our faith? Well, it is not in *what*
we put our faith rather it is in *whom* we place our trust. Jesus has
accomplished salvation for *all* who will simply *believe* (trust) in what
He has done on their behalf. *He* was crushed for our iniquities and
by *His* scourging we are healed (Isaiah 53:5). *He* has rescued us from
darkness and *He* has transferred us into His kingdom (Colossians

1:13). Therefore, we are all sons of God through *faith* in Jesus Christ (Galatians 3:26).

Although mankind continues to find ways to divide people, spiritually speaking there are only two types of people in the world, believers and non-believers. Believers are those that belong to the kingdom of God while unbelievers are those that do not. Notice the criteria for salvation… *to believe*. Those that *believe*, which means trusting Jesus completely, will *not* be judged or condemned, while those that *do not believe* are already judged. Why? It is because *they have not believed* in the name of Jesus. It really is that simple. Despite some religious philosophy that focuses primarily on the sinner and his/her performance, the gospel proclaims salvation for everyone who *believes*.

At times we might hear someone say, "Good people go to heaven and bad people go to hell," but this is a myth and is the antithesis to biblical truth regarding salvation. Heaven is given to those who have *called* on the name of the Lord (Romans 10:13), having placed their *faith* in what Jesus has already accomplished on the cross (John 3:18). God loves us and we can call on Him today. We should not pray someone else's words. God desires to hear from us personally. Cry out to Him today and ask Him to save you and you will begin to experience the spiritual freedom that comes from fully trusting Him for your salvation and eternal security.

Your Faith *Is* Your Righteousness

> Now to the one who works, his wage is not credited as a favor, but as what is due. But to the one who does not work, but *believes* in Him who justifies the ungodly, his *faith* is credited as righteousness. (Romans 4:4–5)

I have to admit that this is one of my favorite passages of scripture. This is primarily because it has helped set me free and given me a greater understanding of what God has done for me. Just for fun, find someone that you know well and that has been a Christian for quite some time. Ask that person if they are *righteous*. Now this is just for fun, so don't lose any friendships over this, but you might be surprised at their answer. There are two very common responses to this question. The person might be *hesitant* to say out loud that they believe that they are righteous or the person may express that they are not *feeling* very righteous (unless you catch them on a really good day). Both responses come from a faulty concept of believing that one's righteousness is derived from his/her actions or performance (which can be defined as doing what is good and avoiding what is not appropriate). For the person that is *hesitant* in announcing their righteousness, they might not want to seem spiritually arrogant. If this is the case, it is because they are connecting their own performance to the term righteousness. For the person not *feeling* especially righteous, again they are focused on how they are living and performing in their life. If they have been slipping in their devotion to God or have drifted into sin, they are not going to *feel* very good about themselves because that is how they have chosen to gauge their level of righteousness.

Today's verse completely eliminates this faulty concept. To the person who does *not* work (for his salvation or righteousness) but *believes* in Him (Jesus) who justifies the ungodly, *his/her faith* is credited as righteousness (verse 5). At this point it would be appropriate for us to stop reading and praise God for *declaring* us righteous by our faith and not by our works. So go ahead and give Him praise.

But to fully appreciate this biblical truth, it's important to understand what righteousness means. Righteousness is the state of being as we *ought* to be. It is a condition *acceptable* to God. Simply put, it is to be *right* with God. This is accomplished by *faith*, by trusting in what Jesus has accomplished for us at the cross. It was for spiritual freedom that Jesus suffered and died so that we can enjoy life and be victorious. It is our responsibility to stand firm and not allow *any* religious yoke to hinder us from obeying this truth (Galatians 5:1). Our *faith* in Jesus puts us in a condition that we were designed to experience. This condition is acceptable to God and makes us right with Him, and it is all accomplished through *faith*. Do you know whom you're going to ask the question? Be kind, but I think it will be an eye-opening experience for you.

Never Ever Disappointed

For the Scripture says, "*Whoever believes in Him will not be disappointed*." For there is no distinction between Jew and Greek; for the same Lord is Lord of all, abounding in riches for all who call on Him; for "*Whoever will call on the name of the Lord will be saved*." (Romans 10:11–13)

Let's look at three things:

1. Whoever believes (trusts) in Jesus will *never* be disappointed. When we trust Christ to dwell in our hearts by *faith* (Ephesians 3:17a), when we *believe* that God will reward us as we seek Him (Hebrews 11:6), and when our salvation and righteousness is received from God by *faith* (John 3:18, Romans 4:5), we will be able to live a life full of spiritual strength and stability. Sadly, it is common for people to have regrets (especially as they get older), but as we dedicate our lives *to* and live *for* Jesus, we can be sure that we will *never* be disappointed.

2. God now makes no distinction between Jews (Israel) and Greeks (the rest of the world). Jesus is the propitiation for the *whole* world (1 John 2:2) and *everyone* who asks *will* receive (Matthew 7:8). God is abounding in riches for *all* who call on His name. The separation between God and man has been *dissolved* through the cross of Jesus. He has become our Mediator (1 Timothy 2:5) and God now desires that *all* mankind be saved and come to the knowl-

edge of the truth (1 Timothy 2:4). God is *not* one to show partiality rather whoever *believes* in Him *has* forgiveness of sins (Acts 10:34, 43).

3. *Whoever* calls of the name of the Lord will be saved (verse 13). If we were to read the very next verse in this passage (Romans 10:14) we would discover a rational and practical look at why believers should share their experience in Jesus with others. How is someone going to *call* on God to be saved if they do not believe in Him in the first place? How can they *believe* the good news of Jesus if they have never heard about it? And how are they supposed to hear about it, unless someone tells them? Some translations use the word "preacher" in this verse but the word is really referring to anyone who will *proclaim* the truth of the gospel. This is not just specifying someone who stands in a pulpit. When we see a really great movie, isn't one of the first things we do is tell someone else about it? When we eat in a really fantastic restaurant, don't we usually recommend it to others? But when God saves us and blesses us beyond anything we could ever deserve, are we quick to tell someone else? Knowing that as we trust in Jesus we will never be disappointed, understanding that there is now no distinction between people groups, and acknowledging the importance of sharing our faith with others, why not share the good news of Jesus with someone today!

Petition #3:
The Importance of Love

Love As Strength

"Being rooted and grounded in *love*" (Ephesians 3:17b).

In the Christian life, love is everything. Let's take a biblical look at love and why the Bible describes love as an imperative for those who follow Jesus.

The strength of a tree is not in its branches rather its stability comes from its root system. The deeper and thicker the roots; the greater capacity the tree has for withstanding anything that might come against it. Likewise, the more that a Christian experiences the love of God in his/her life, the more likely that individual will be equipped to love others, overcoming the obstacles that a loveless attitude so often brings. Today's passage describes a life that draws its strength from love found within. These two words, *rooted* and *grounded*, convey the idea of stability and strength. To be rooted or grounded means to be firm or fixed in place. It is to be established so that one cannot be shaken. This is what love does for the believer in Jesus. Since the first fruit of the Spirit is *love* (Galatians 5:22), it should not be a surprise that the prayer we are studying begins with a petition to God for strength in the inner man through *His* Spirit and then goes on to describe this stability (rooting and grounding) as coming from love. Love is a stabilizing force. Without it, you can have religion, but you cannot have Christian authenticity. Jesus reminds us that our love is to be different from the way the world loves. It is not difficult to love those who love us in return (family, friends, etc.), but the believer's capacity to love reaches far beyond those relationships into the lives of those who are demanding and difficult (Matthew 5:46–47). For the Christian, love really *is* everything. Pray and ask God to fill you with *His* love so that you can love others and effectively represent Christ to a lost and dying world.

The Litmus Test for
Christian Authenticity

"Beloved, let us *love* one another, for *love* is from
God; and everyone who *loves* is born of God and
knows God. The one who does *not love* does not
know God, *for God is love*" (1 John 4:7–8).

Today's passage is a clear and succinct reminder of the importance of
experiencing the love of God in our lives. God *is* love. Perhaps that
is one of the most important statements made in all of scripture.
Whatever other characteristics we attach to our understanding about
our Creator, the reality that He *is* love must not be ignored or dimin-
ished. Let's look at the amazing truths found in today's passage.

First, there is a plea for us to love one another. The word *agape*
(love) is used in the New Testament more than two hundred times.
With even a cursory reading of the Bible, it is difficult to miss the
theme that loving others is at the core of the Christian experience.
Why? It is because love is *from* God. Our capacity to receive and give
love is by His design. It only stands to reason that a God who *is* love
would create beings with that same ability. Love brings stability, love
creates security, and love promotes spiritual prosperity. To experience
love and acceptance is by God's design. Secondly, everyone who loves
demonstrates two important things.

1. Christian love affirms one's salvation. "Everyone who
   loves *is* born of God" (John 3:3). Once again, this is the
   capacity to love others *beyond* our family and friends

(Matthew 5:46–47). This is a supernatural ability to love others in the face of anger, hostility, and hatred. As Jesus was facing the torment and ridicule associated with the cross, He was still able to love by praying, "Father, forgive them, for they do not know what they are doing" (Luke 23:34). Likewise, Stephen, while being persecuted, as the crowd was stoning Him, was able to say, "Lord, do not hold this sin against them" (Acts 7:60). Those that love this way prove themselves to be "born of God."

2. Christian love affirms that we *know* God. Once again, it only stands to reason that if God *is* love, then our capacity to love would testify to our knowledge of Him. This type of knowledge goes far beyond knowing *about* God rather it is relational experience *with* God. Conversely, the opposite is true. "The one who does *not* love does *not* know God because God *is* love." How we treat others usually indicates how we view God. Our passage today leaves little room for us to profess an intimate relationship with God while cursing the very people around us. Love is the litmus test for Christian authenticity. As you pray today, ask someone close to you how you measure up to this passage. If you fall short, ask God for a fresh filling of His love in your life so that you can supernaturally love those around you.

The Absence of Love

> If I speak with the tongues of men and of angels, but do not have *love*, I have become a noisy gong or a clanging cymbal. If I have the gift of prophecy and know all mysteries and all knowledge; and if I have all faith, so as to remove mountains, but do not have *love*, I am nothing. And if I give all my possessions to feed the poor, and if I surrender my body to be burned, but do not have *love*, it profits me nothing. (1 Corinthians 13:1–3)

Today's passage comes out of what is often called the love chapter. Perhaps you have heard it quoted in a wedding or other event. It has a very significant message for everyone who claims the name of Jesus. Not only is love the litmus test for Christian authenticity, it is essential that love is the motive for anything we say, believe, or do.

First, "If I speak but do not love, I have become a noisy gong or clanging cymbal" (verse 1). Words are important. They can build up or tear down, convey encouragement or create despair. In short, words communicate either life or death. We are reminded that praising God in one breath while cursing others with the next is *loveless* speech and has no place in the life of a believer (James 3:9). Our speech should be void of anything worthless and unproductive rather our words should be edifying (building up), laced with grace (joy, sweetness, and goodwill), and should promote growth in others (Ephesians 4:29). If we think we are faithful in our belief, yet cannot bridle our tongues, we deceive ourselves and our religion has become worthless (James 1:26).

Secondly, "If I have the gift of prophecy, if I know all mysteries, if I possess all knowledge, if I have all faith but do not have love, I am nothing" (verse 2). That's quite a list! Anything we know or believe, without love as the driving force, is of no value. Gifting, knowledge, and faith are all important parts of the Christian life, however, without love, they do not promote the gospel and render us ineffective. In order to succeed, the world tells us that we need to be the most intelligent, knowledgeable, and talented people. However, Jesus reminds us that unless we are converted (born again) and become *like* children, we will not enter the kingdom of heaven (Matthew 18:3). This is not acting childish or being a baby, it is the state of a grateful, trusting heart, full of love for God and others. In addition, Jesus reminds us that the greatest in *His* kingdom are those who humble themselves *like* a child (Matthew 18:4). This childlike heart is pleasing to God, promotes godly love, and should be in every believer.

Finally, this passage reminds us that no matter what we do, without love, there is no profit in the effort. "If I give all of my possessions to feed the poor, and if I surrender my body to be burned, but do not have love, it profits me *nothing*" (verse 3). Mankind only sees the works of others but God searches beyond our actions into our hearts to examine the motives behind our endeavors. Whatever we say, whatever we believe, and whatever we do, if love is not the motive, we waste our time. Said another way: "Let all that you do be done in love" (1 Corinthians 16:14).

Love Is the Fulfillment of the Law

> Owe nothing to anyone except to *love* one another;
> for he who *loves* his neighbor has *fulfilled the*
> *law*. For this, "*You shall not commit adultery, you*
> *shall not murder, you shall not steal, you shall not*
> *covet*," and if there is any other commandment,
> it is summed up in this saying, "*You shall love*
> *your neighbor as yourself*." *Love* does no wrong to
> a neighbor; therefore *love is the fulfillment of the*
> *law*. (Romans 13:8–10)

I have to admit that this is another one of those passages that has
had a profound effect on my spiritual life. Certainly the Bible speaks
against legalism in the life of the believer but even if we were to have
an interest in following the letter of the Law, it can be summed up in
love. There are three statements made in today's passage, and they all
point to a single truth: that love *fulfills* the Law of God.

First, do not owe anything to anyone except to *love* them. When
we love our neighbor, we have fulfilled the Law. Notice it doesn't say
that if you love your neighbor "you're on your way to fulfilling the
Law" or "you're taking a step in the right direction in fulfilling the
Law." "He who loves his neighbor *has* fulfilled the Law." Mission
accomplished! Of course none of us love perfectly all of the time, but
this passage reminds us where our focus should be. Christians should
always be looking for ways to redeem relationships through a patient
attitude, gentle speech, and kind actions. Patience, gentleness, and
kindness are not only *descriptions* of love, they are also *attributes* of
the fruit of the Spirit of God. Said another way, people living by the

guidance of the Holy Spirit will exhibit these characteristics in their day-to-day activities, fulfilling the Law and purposes of God.

Secondly, any commandment can be summed up in *loving* others. This is what Jesus was teaching when He was asked which commandment was the most important. Jesus said that *loving* God and *loving* others was at the heart of the Law and that *all* of the Law and the Prophets (writings in the Old Testament) could be *summed up* in those two commandments (Matthew 22:36–40). Today's passage echoes that truth. Adultery, murder, stealing, coveting, and any other commandment can be summed up in *loving* others like we *love* ourselves (Matthew 7:12).

Finally, love does no wrong to anyone. Three descriptions consistent with *agape* (love) are affection, goodwill, and benevolence. If we love people, we must have a positive *disposition* toward them. If we love people, we should *desire* to see good come into their life. And if we love people, we should be willing to *do* what is necessary to help them in whatever capacity that implies.

He who loves His neighbor *has* fulfilled the Law. All of the commandments can be summed up in *loving* others. Therefore, love *is* the fulfillment of the Law. Let's go out, love others, and fulfill the Law of God today!

Recognizable Christianity

A new commandment I give to you, that you *love* one another, even as I have *loved* you, that you also *love* one another. By this all men will *know* that you are My disciples, if you have *love* for one another. (John 13:34–35)

Here is a thought from our Lord: when we love each other, the world will recognize us as believers. Unlike the old covenant with its ordinances and statutes, Jesus gives the church a *new* commandment: to love one another. Jesus then uses His own sacrificial love (even prior to the cross) as a standard by which we too are to love. Don't forget that God *is* love. The litmus test for Christian authenticity and one's ability to fulfill the Law of God is rooted, grounded, and centered in love. Because Jesus has loved us by providing salvation to everyone who will call on His name (Romans 10:13), we too are to love in that very same manner (1 John 4:7–11). Love is what makes Christians recognizable to the rest of the world.

It should come as no surprise that our enemy, the accuser of the saved, would want to disrupt the church to the point that love for one another is nonexistent. Not just for the purpose of seeing believers at each other's throats but also knowing that an absence of love will make it impossible for the world to recognize the church as being *of* God. Perhaps that's why believers are instructed not to *grieve* the Holy Spirit. Bitterness, wrath, anger, slander, and malice are all works of the enemy and do not belong in the life of a Christian (Ephesians 4:30–31).

Rather, love, joy, peace, patience, kindness, goodness, faithfulness, gentleness, and self-control are the fruits that come from a born-again, Spirit-filled life (Galatians 5:22–23). Let's love one another so that *all* mankind will know that we are disciples of Jesus!

Petition #4:
Intimately Knowing the
Love of Christ

The Love of God

"And to *know* the love of Christ which surpasses *knowledge*" (Ephesians 3:19a).

Have you ever noticed that God's Word makes statements that defy human logic and reason? "The last will be first and the first will be last" (Matthew 20:16). "Whoever wishes to save his life will lose it but whoever loses his life for the sake of Christ will find it" (Luke 9:24). "God has chosen foolish things to shame the wise and the weak things to shame the strong" (1 Corinthians 1:27). God's ways really are higher than ours (Isaiah 55:9).

Today's passage is another one of those statements. We are praying to *know* the love of Christ, which *surpasses* knowledge. I believe the key to understanding this statement is simple. God wants you to know His love *relationally*, meaning to know Him through *experience*. This love *surpasses* knowledge because it cannot be arrived at through human, intellectual pursuit alone. The love of Christ is to be enjoyed, not just studied. God has chosen, through the gospel, to reveal Himself to those who *believe*. We do not obtain a relationship with God through intellectual wisdom alone rather it is attained through *faith* (1 Corinthians 1:21). He has chosen to reveal

Himself to those who will simply trust Him with a child-like faith (Matthew 11:25).

We can *study* manuals on how to drive or we can get in a car and *actually* drive. We can *read* reviews of the latest movie or we can go to the theater and *see* the movie for ourselves. Likewise, we can study *about* God's love or we can *experience* it. The latter is far more rewarding than the former.

Pray and ask God to reveal His love to you. Perhaps you have never really experienced the love of God in your life. Maybe you just need a fresh filling of God's love. Whichever the case, be open to what God has to say to you as we look at a love which surpasses human, intellectual knowledge.

The love of God is greater far than tongue or pen can ever tell;
It goes beyond the highest star, and reaches to the lowest hell;
The guilty pair, bowed down with care, God gave His Son to win;
His erring child He reconciled and pardoned from his sin.
Could we with ink the ocean fill, and were
the skies of parchment made,
Were every stalk on earth a quill, and every man a scribe by trade;
To write the love of God above would drain the ocean dry;
Nor could the scroll contain the whole,
though stretched from sky to sky.

—Frederick M. Lehman, 1917

In Accordance with Knowledge

> Brethren, my heart's desire and my prayer to God for them is for their salvation. For I testify about them that they have a zeal for God, but not in accordance with *knowledge*. For not *knowing* about God's righteousness and seeking to establish their own, they did not subject themselves to the righteousness of God. For Christ is the end of the law for righteousness to everyone who believes. (Romans 10:1–4)

Praying for someone's salvation is a noble pursuit. That is exactly what today's passage is all about. A man named Paul is interceding for his fellow Jewish brethren, and he is praying for their salvation. Having met the Person of Jesus Christ, Paul, a man who formerly promoted Jewish Law, has now obtained relational knowledge about God previously veiled to him. His encounter with Jesus brought a new understanding regarding God and His provision of salvation through faith. The testimony about his fellow Jewish friends is that they had a *zeal* for God. To be zealous is to be eager and enthusiastic about a cause. It is having an intense desire to accomplish a task. They had *zeal* for God but not according to *knowledge*. So what was the problem? Our passage points out three areas of misunderstanding.

1. They did not *know* about God's righteousness. They were still operating under the idea that adherence to the Law of Moses was how an individual would be justified before God. This misunderstanding led to the second problem.

41

2. They were seeking to *establish* their own righteousness. Establishing our own righteousness is to focus on our *behavior* as a gauge for determining whether our justification is warranted. When someone is ignorant about the truth that a man is only justified by *faith* in Jesus, works-based religions can become very attractive. A religious person will often attempt to *gain* God's approval through his/her actions. This leads to the last problem.

3. Therefore, seeking to establish their own righteousness, they did not *subject* themselves to the righteousness of God (by faith). *"For Christ is the end (culmination) of the law for righteousness to everyone who believes"* (verse 4). A lack of understanding this important truth leads to substituting our own ideas and efforts in place of God's provision causing a failure to receive the gift of salvation by faith. Jesus's death on the cross, established a new covenant with mankind, thus making the old covenant null and void (Hebrews 8:13, 2 Corinthians 3:6). A desire to please God (zeal) is not enough. That enthusiasm needs to be accompanied by proper *knowledge* regarding salvation. It is vital that we, as believers, understand that our righteousness is credited to us by *faith* and that this righteousness is attributed to us *apart* from works (Romans 4:5–6). Is *your* zeal in accordance with knowledge?

Saving Knowledge

> Nevertheless *knowing* that a man is not justified by the works of the Law but through faith in Christ Jesus, even we have believed in Christ Jesus, so that we may be justified by faith in Christ and not by the works of the Law; since by the works of the Law no flesh will be justified.
> (Galatians 2:16)

Let's take a look at the knowledge necessary for us to accurately understand the issue of eternal salvation. This saving knowledge is summarized in today's passage. Two important truths are found in this verse. Mankind is *not* justified by works of the Law rather mankind *is* justified by faith in Jesus Christ. The essence of being *justified* is being "as one ought to be." It is a state of *rightness* before God. Consider the repetition Paul uses in explaining justification. Three times Paul repeats how mankind is *not* justified before God. Consider the following statements:

"A man is *not* justified by works of the Law"
"*Not* by works of the Law"
"By works of the Law *no* flesh will be justified."

"Works of the Law" can be understood as doing the things one *should* do and *avoiding* the things that God finds unacceptable. It is hard to imagine anyone coming away from this passage believing that "works of the Law" play a role in justification.

But just in case we have missed Paul's appeal for us to have *faith* in Jesus as the means for our justification, three times he repeats how mankind *is* made right with God. Again, consider the following statements:

"Through *faith* in Christ Jesus"
"Even we have *believed* in Christ Jesus"
"So that we may be justified by *faith* in Christ."

Notice that the faith exhibited by the believer is *in* Jesus. The object of our faith is as important as the faith itself. Under the new covenant, God has chosen to save everyone who believes *in* Jesus and puts their trust *in* what He has accomplished on the cross for them. This process of being justified is completely *apart* from works performed by the saved individual.

I often wonder how much spiritual suffering occurs in the lives of believers simply because of the faulty concept that justification is somehow in their hands. Proclaiming the truth found in this passage is a vital part of accurately explaining the gospel (good news) to others. *Knowing* that *"a man is not justified by works of the Law but through faith in Christ Jesus"* is also essential for enjoying spiritual freedom in our lives!

Let It Be Known

> Therefore let it be *known* to you, brethren, that through Him (Jesus) *forgiveness* of sins is proclaimed to you, and through Him (Jesus) everyone who believes is *freed* from all things, from which you could not be *freed* through the Law of Moses. (Acts 13:38–39)

In today's passage, we see two foundational pillars of the Christian faith: *forgiveness* and *freedom*. These two concepts are also connected. An individual's spiritual freedom is connected to his/her willingness to forgive. Likewise, those who find joy and fulfillment in Christ are much more equipped to forgive others around them. The declaration is "let it be *known*." Let it be known that in Jesus Christ, there is *forgiveness* of sins—*all* of them. We are designed to live in forgiveness. Show me a life full of struggle and I will show you someone who needs to experience or give *forgiveness*. Forgiveness is a *release* of any possible penalty being issued for an offense. That is why scripture says that we are *blessed* when our sins are covered (forgiven) apart from works (Romans 4:6). There are three areas of our lives that will be positively or negatively impacted depending on the presence or lack of forgiveness.

1. We need forgiveness *from* God. There is no fear in love rather God's perfect love drives out fear from our lives because fear is associated with punishment (1 John 4:18). Those who fear punishment for their sins have not experienced the complete forgiveness that Jesus died to provide.

2. We need to forgive *others*. Jesus teaches the importance of forgiveness by instructing us to forgive as many times as necessary (Matthew 18:22). He also tells us that an unwillingness to forgive blocks the possibility of experiencing God's forgiveness (Matthew 6:14–15).

3. We need to forgive *ourselves*. This is often the most difficult part of experiencing forgiveness. Christians who cannot seem to forgive themselves are really ignoring what Jesus has accomplished on the cross on their behalf. Rather than wallow around in despair over our mistakes, we should talk to God about our sin and experience forgiveness from Him (1 John 1:9).

Also, let it be known that in a relationship with Jesus, we are freed from *all* things. Mankind has been efficient in adding to the gospel of Jesus. It is often difficult for people to accept God's love and forgiveness without attaching conditions to it. But scripture is quite clear that salvation, forgiveness, and freedom are for *everyone* who *believes*. Everyone who *believes* will *not* perish but *have* eternal life (John 3:16). Everyone who *believes* is *not* condemned (John 3:18). For everyone who *believes*, his/her faith is credited *as* righteousness (Romans 4:5). The gospel has the power to save everyone who *believes* (Romans 1:16). The greatness of God's power is toward everyone who *believes* (Ephesians 1:18–19). And it is the will of the Father that everyone who beholds the Son (Jesus) and *believes* in Him, that they will have eternal life and Jesus Himself will raise them up on the last day (John 6:40).

These are just some of the powerful truths about receiving forgiveness and freedom by *faith*. It is important to note that this freedom is found in a relationship with Jesus and is not possible through the Law of Moses. Substituting law keeping for resting in the finished work of the cross does not bring about spiritual freedom. Legalism makes it *more* difficult for us to enjoy freedom in Christ. Consequently because forgiveness and freedom are connected, a lack of spiritual freedom can lead to our failing to forgiving others, even ourselves. As you pray today, ask God for forgiveness and freedom in your life and ask Him to give you the opportunity to "let it be known!"

The Knowledge of the Truth

> This is good and acceptable in the sight of God our Savior, who desires all men to be saved and to come to the *knowledge* of the truth. For there is one God, and one mediator also between God and men, the man Christ Jesus, who gave Himself as a ransom for all, the testimony given at the proper time. (1 Timothy 2:3–6)

We have been looking at what it means to know the love of Christ, which surpasses knowledge. This knowledge is relational, as opposed to merely being intellectual. This knowledge includes *knowing* that mankind is justified through faith in Jesus and not by works of the Law. This knowledge encompasses having zeal for God but in accordance with the understanding that experiencing God's love is through faith. This knowledge, that salvation, forgiveness, and spiritual freedom are available by faith in Jesus, is to be proclaimed to everyone (Mark 16:15).

Our passage today tells us that God desires all mankind to be saved and to come to this life giving, saving knowledge. The word being used in this passage for "men" can be translated mankind and literally means "humans." The idea being conveyed in this passage is that God is *willing* for all mankind to be saved. For God did not send Jesus for the *condemnation* of the world rather that the world might be *saved* through Him (John 3:17). So just as sin came to all mankind through the one act of disobedience in Adam, the one act of righteousness by Jesus on the cross brings justification of life to all mankind (Romans 5:18). So why doesn't everyone receive salvation through Jesus? The Bible informs us of two things that prohibit this transformation.

1. Our spiritual enemy is working against the gospel by trying to conceal it from humanity (2 Corinthians 4:3–4). Jesus teaches this in the Parable of the Sower (Matthew 13:19, Mark 4:15, Luke 8:12). The "god of this world" is referring to Satan (who is our adversary), also described as the evil one and the devil, meaning slanderer. Scripture tells us that he works to keep the gospel out of the hearts of the unsaved so that they will not come to the knowledge of the truth. No wonder he stirs up so many divisions in the church, knowing that it is the church's main mission to preach and teach the good news.

2. The second obstacle to salvation is mankind himself. When the gospel is preached, it is often ignored or resisted simply because the hearer prefers to live life on his/her own terms. Light (Jesus) has come into the world but mankind loves darkness (their sin) more than they love the Light (John 3:19). Many refuse to come because they do not want to give an account to anyone about how they live their lives. Ironically, they will anyway. As believers it is our responsibility to share the love of Jesus with everyone. We should care for our neighbor's salvation as much as we care for our own. God desires all mankind to be saved and to come to the knowledge of truth. Why not spread that knowledge today!

Petition #5:
Living Abundant Lives

The Fullness of God

"That you may be *filled up* to all the *fullness* of God" (Ephesians 3:19b).

Today let's take a look at what it means to live in the *fullness* of God. To be *filled up* is to be spiritually filled to the brim. It is to be supplied liberally and to have a spiritual *abundance*. The world often defines abundance by the material possessions that we have but, for the believer, abundance goes way beyond material things into the very heart of the individual. "To be filled up to all the fullness of God" is a truly remarkable statement. As human beings, having been redeemed by faith in Jesus, we can actually experience this fullness in our daily lives, regardless of our economic status. God is able to do far more *abundantly* beyond anything we could ever ask or imagine (Ephesians 3:20). He is *abounding* in riches for all who call on His name (Romans 10:12). Our heavenly Father will *lavishly* give what is good to those who ask (Matthew 7:11). In fact, our lives are to *overflow* with God's fullness. Consider Jesus's words:

"He who believes in Me, as the Scripture said, 'From his innermost being will *flow* rivers of living water'" (John 7:38).

Notice that this living water comes from our *innermost* being, and it is to *flow* out of us and into the lives of others. Are you being filled up to all of the fullness of God? Does your life overflow with rivers of living water?

There are many things that can stand in the way of living this type of life. Depression, despair, failure, broken relationships, guilt, shame, and physical problems are just a few of the struggles that can cause us to live short of spiritual *fullness*. Take your Bible and review the different elements of the prayer we have been studying (Ephesians 3:16–19, the entire prayer is found in verses 14–21). As we ask God to strengthen us by His Spirit, when Jesus sits on the throne of our hearts, as we are rooted and grounded in love for God and others, and as we experience the love of Christ in our own lives, *then* we will be filled up to all the fullness of God. We will live in abundance and become spiritual fountains for all in the world to see. Trust God in every aspect of your life and start living in abundance today!

Grace Abounding

"The Law came in so that the transgression would increase; but where sin increased, grace *abounded* all the more" (Romans 5:20).

In recent years, I've noticed our culture's fascination with superhero movies. I have to admit that I have seen my fair share of them too. So why do these movies appeal to us? I believe one reason is that we like seeing the superhero defend humanity against the evil that is wreaking havoc on society. Although these movies are fictional, deep down inside we know our world is broken and that we are powerless to change the situation. We need a hero—a superhero.

Our passage today expresses what our hearts long to believe, that the suffering and brokenness of this world is *redeemable*, that there is something capable of reversing the course of human sinfulness. Well there is—it is God's *grace*.

First, we need to establish that the purpose of the Law is not to create a viable way for us to be made right with God. Truthfully, it is quite the opposite. The Law was given so that our transgressions (our sinfulness) would *increase*. Increase? I thought the Law was good? The Law *is* good because it is God's perfect design for how we should live; however, none of us are capable of living up to that standard. This is the key to understanding our problem and appreciating the solution. Sin is our problem. It is what keeps us apart from God. Satan is our spiritual enemy, and he knows this all too well. He traffics in guilt, shame, condemnation, depression, despair, and ultimately spiritual destruction. When we believe that we need to become *better* people, we play right into his hand. The Bible reminds us of three very important things regarding the Law.

1. If we have broken *any* of God's Law, we are guilty of violating the entire thing (James 2:10). God does not judge on the curve, nor does He compare our lives with the lives of others. We are all *equally* in need of a Savior.
2. The Law was *never* given to make us complete (Galatians 2:21, 3:21). If it were possible for us to live a life worthy of God, then Jesus's sacrifice on the cross would become meaningless and entirely unnecessary. When we assess our standing with God by our works, we are, perhaps unintentionally, making that declaration about Christ.
3. The Law was designed to demonstrate our *need* for a Savior (Galatians 3:24). Just like in the superhero movie, humanity is incapable of saving themselves and is in need of God's intervention. So the *bad* news (we are all sinful and in need of salvation) leads us to the *good* news (that Jesus has accomplished our salvation apart from works).

Secondly, we need to rightly compare God's grace to our need. Where sin increased, grace *abounds* all the more. To abound is to go beyond, to exceed one's expectations. It is an overflow of abundance. It is really hard to encapsulate the meaning of this word. Whatever we say about abounding, it goes beyond even that. I have a passion for declaring this truth primarily because I have spent too much of my life believing (falsely) that my sin was somehow more powerful in *defeating* me than God's grace is in *rescuing* me. I know there are others who feel the same way because I have heard the all too familiar expressions of this false belief from them. "You just don't know the things I've done." "God couldn't possibly forgive me for that." "If I walk into the church, I'm afraid the walls would cave in around me." These are all expressions of a powerful but false belief that our sin is greater than the grace of God. The enemy would love to keep us in that place but the truth is that wherever sin increases, God's grace super abounds! Jesus came that the world might be saved through

Him (John 3:17). He is the atoning sacrifice for the sins of the whole world (1 John 2:2). His grace is capable of *exceeding* our expectations. His grace allows us to live in victory and assurance, and His grace is but a prayer away (Romans 10:13). Wherever sin increases, grace *abounds* all the more!

An Uncommon Life

"The thief comes only to steal and kill and destroy; I came that they may have life and have it *abundantly*" (John 10:10).

Our passage today expresses God's desire to not only give us life but for us to live life *abundantly*. We have a spiritual enemy who wants nothing less than to rob us of the abundant life that Jesus has purchased for us. This spiritual enemy steals—in all sorts of ways. He wants to steal our assurance. He desires to steal our peace. And he will attempt to convince us that an abundant life in God is unachievable. Stealing, by definition, is taking something that does not belong to you. Our assurance, peace, and abundance in Jesus belong to *us*. The only way the enemy can take from us spiritually is if we allow him to do so. Just like locking our houses while we are away, we have to guard our minds and hearts against anything that might give the enemy a foothold. He desires to kill and destroy anyone that he can. I believe that is why we are reminded to be on guard with all diligence in our spiritual lives (1 Peter 5:8–9).

Unlike the enemy, Jesus came to *give* us life and for us to have it *abundantly*. Abundance in this passage means over and above, more than is necessary, superior, extraordinary, and uncommon. This type of life is not only rewarding for us, but also allows us to testify to the goodness of God. Our life in Christ manifests itself in a number of ways. As Christians, we are able to *reject* the ways of the world (1 John 2:15–17), living by *faith* in Jesus, and *trusting* His purpose for our lives (Galatians 2:20). We set our minds on things above rather than on earthly things (Colossians 3:2). We seek God's kingdom and

His righteousness, knowing that as we make Christ our priority, He supplies everything else that we need (Matthew 6:33). These attitudes reflect a changed life and I believe this is why we should pray and ask, "To be filled up to all the fullness of God" (Ephesians 3:19).

Section 1: Transforming Your Prayer Life: Ephesians 3:14–21

Epilogue

We need to rid our lives of sin, guilt, doubt, dead religion, bad doctrine, and anything else that might stand in the way of realizing the fullness of God and truly living an uncommon life. As you move on to the next section of this book, I would like to encourage you to continue praying through the five petitions found in this prayer. Continue to meditate on the truths found in each passage and share this knowledge with others. If you are studying in a small group, stay connected to those in the group. Consider beginning the next study together. I hope that you find yourself spiritually stronger than when you began. Continue to pray and seek God's forgiveness, grace, and abundance as you carry on in your walk with Christ!

> Now to Him who is able to do far more abundantly beyond all that we ask or think, according to the power that works within us, to Him be the glory in the church and in Christ Jesus to all generations forever and ever. Amen. (Ephesians 3:20–21)

SECTION 2

Reading through the Gospel of Matthew

Introduction: The Story Of Christ

Are you ready to go on a twenty-eight-day challenge? This section is entitled, "Reading through the Gospel of Matthew" and will provide you with the opportunity to read through an entire gospel in just four weeks. Each day, you will be directed to read one chapter of this tremendous gospel. In addition, we will be spotlighting one specific passage from that chapter. This will allow for a more in-depth examination and discussion of the text. Here are my recommendations for getting the most from your study:

1. If possible, recruit a few others to walk through the study with you.
2. Print out each passage of scripture and post it in a prominent place in your home (refrigerator, bathroom mirror, etc.)
3. Make discussion of each passage a priority for the group.

Our Overarching Goals:

To read the entire gospel in just four weeks!
To have a better understanding of the truths found in the Gospel of Matthew!
To meditate on these truths, strengthening us in our daily lives!
May God richly bless you as you begin your journey!

What's in a Name?

"She will bear a Son; and you shall call His name *Jesus*, for He will save His people from their sins" (Matthew 1:21).

Today: Read Matthew 1

Chapter 1 brings us three important aspects regarding the identity and Person of Jesus Christ. But before we look at that, I want to encourage you not to skip past the genealogy found at the beginning of this gospel. Take some time and appreciate the forty-two generations described in this list, outlining the lineage of Christ from Abraham to David and ultimately to Jesus Himself. You may also notice names like Rahab, Tamar, Ruth, and Bathsheba, all of which were Gentile women and some whose names are associated with scandalous situations. This introduction to Matthew reminds me that although humanity is fallen and that we often make mistakes, God is able to take our misdeeds and weave them into a wonderful tapestry of redemption. So if we find ourselves in a family that is broken, blended, or battle-weary, let this portion of scripture remind you of God's grace and forgiveness.

What is it that sets the Christian faith apart from the rest of the religious and philosophical thinking of our day? The answer: the Person of Jesus Christ. Most, if not all other beliefs systems, recognize Jesus as a prophet, teacher, historical figure, or moral person, but they all stop short of recognizing Jesus as who He is: the very Son of God. So what's in a name? Everything when it comes to Jesus!

Our passage today teaches us three important aspects regarding the identity of Christ.

1. Twice, we are told, that Jesus was conceived by the Holy Spirit (verses 18, 20). Born of the virgin Mary, Jesus's conception was different from any other person that has ever walked the earth. He was actually conceived by God's Spirit. Considering the gravity of this news, Jesus's earthly father, Joseph, had to be told by way of an angelic visit. Authentic Christian faith will always include an acknowledgement that Jesus is the Son of God (1 John 4:15).

2. Joseph was instructed to name the child *Jesus*, "for He will save His people from their sins" (verse 21). The name *Jesus* literally means "God saves." That is why we *pray* in His name and that is why there is *power* in His name. Every time we utter the name of Jesus, we are declaring the saving power of God.

3. Finally, we are reminded that the prophet Isaiah had foretold that the child would also be called *Immanuel* (verse 23, sometimes spelled Emmanuel). Immanuel means "God with us." As we read through Matthew, remember that every occasion in which Jesus is teaching is an opportunity because He is Immanuel, for us to hear directly from our Creator. When Jesus speaks, God Himself is speaking.

So let's celebrate Jesus! He *is* the Son of God (John 1:14). His name reverberates the truth about the saving power of God (Romans 1:16). And as Immanuel, we are reminded that He *is* God (John 1:1). He has been given the name that is above all names, that at the name of Jesus, every knee will bow and every tongue will confess that Jesus Christ is Lord to the glory of God the Father (Philippians 2:10–11).

Elusive Joy

"When they saw the star, they rejoiced *exceedingly*
with great joy" (Matthew 2:10).

Today: Read Matthew 2

Joy is an amazing thing! It puts a little click in our step and a twinkle
in our eye. It motivates us to press on and meet each new day with a
renewed vigor. The power of joy is truly amazing! Today we find the
magi following the star in order to see the Christ-child. They were
bearing gifts and ready to worship Jesus. Upon seeing the star, our
passage tells us that they *rejoiced*. The word rejoiced has within it the
concept of joy. So it would be accurate to say that the magi were full
of joy, thus they were *rejoicing*. But that's not all. They were rejoicing
exceedingly. This word ramps up the type of joy they were experiencing. This was not ordinary rather they were experiencing a joy that
could not be contained. But that's *still* not all. The passage tells us
that they were rejoicing exceedingly with *great* joy. I find it amazing
that scripture uses three separate descriptors to define the magi's joy:
rejoicing, exceedingly, and with great joy.

So do you, as a Christian, experience this type of joy? I would
love to say that every day I am like the magi, but that would not
be true. Sometimes joy seems elusive. How about you? Why do we
sometimes come up short of rejoicing exceedingly with great joy?
While there can be all kinds of physical, emotional, mental, and spiritual factors, I want to suggest three things that can rob us of our joy.

1. Lack of assurance of your salvation. I cannot count the number of people that struggle with a lack of knowing that they are saved. While this does not manifest itself in the life of every believer, it is no surprise that it *does* take place. As Christians, we are not just saved from our sin and eternal separation from God, we have been declared children of God and heirs to His kingdom (Romans 8:16–17). But we have a spiritual enemy that wants to rob us of the joy that comes *with* salvation. He traffics in doubt, which is the opposite of faith. This is why it is so important not to attach our works to the issue of salvation. Everyone who calls on the name of the Lord *will* be saved (Romans 10:13). Whoever believes (trusts) in Jesus is *not* judged (John 3:18). There is now *no* condemnation for those who are in Christ Jesus (Romans 8:1). Call on God, ask Him to save you, be baptized as a public witness to your faith, and then rest on the promises of God for your salvation.

2. Holding on to past sin. The past is the past. We cannot go back and change anything that has happened there. It is truly a waste of time to *dwell* on past experiences. As believers, we are assured that as we confess our sin to God, He is faithful and just to forgive us of our sin (1 John 1:9). But again, we have a spiritual enemy that would want nothing less than to steal our joy by continually reminding us of our mistakes. The apostle Paul reminds us of the importance of forgetting what is behind us and pressing on toward what is ahead (Philippians 3:13–14). We are to approach His throne of grace with confidence, trusting in God's grace and mercy (Hebrews 4:16). At one point, Jesus instructed Peter to forgive as many times as was necessary (Matthew 18:21–22). God is willing to do the same. When we confess our sin to Him and leave it there, we can be assured that He will cast it away as far as the east is from the west (Psalm 103:3,12).

3. Not using our gifts within the church. As Christians, each of us has been gifted with abilities that only we can accom-

plish for the kingdom (1 Corinthians 12:4–7). Not everyone has the same gifts, but each of us is to use those gifts for the building up of the church, which is the manifestation of the kingdom of God here on earth. We are designed to live with purpose. Satan would love to convince us that we are not *worthy* to serve. He will use guilt, fear of failure, and any other lie he can come up with just as long as he can keep us from fulfilling our God-given purpose. We should all ask God to direct us as to what He desires for us to accomplish for His kingdom and then begin living with that purpose in mind.

One final thought. I believe that many people have a faulty idea of church. Figuratively, we could argue that the magi were on their way to *church* since they were seeking the One who gives the church its reason to exist in the first place. For many, church is something to be endured rather than something to be celebrated. Gathering together with other believers should bring us joy. Bible study, prayer, and spending time with God should not be thought of as a duty rather a privilege. The second fruit listed as coming from God's Spirit is joy (Galatians 5:22). As believers, joy is an indispensable part of life. As we study Matthew together, may our joy be ever increasing so that we all, like the magi, can rejoice exceedingly with great joy!

Godly Fuel

"As for me, I baptize you with water for repentance, but He who is coming after me is mightier than I, and I am not fit to remove His sandals; He will baptize you with the *Holy Spirit* and fire" (Matthew 3:11).

Today: Read Matthew 3

John the Baptist was sent to work on behalf of God prior to Jesus's earthly ministry. Our passage today informs us that part of this work was to baptize people for repentance while waiting on the greater work that God would do after Jesus's earthly life. This *greater* work would be accomplished by the sending of the Holy Spirit to assist every believer. Repentance is defined as "changing one's mind." When we come to Jesus, we do so on the basis of what Christ has already done for us by becoming our atoning sacrifice. Baptism then follows as an outward testimony of that inward change. But this is just the beginning of the Christian life. For the rest of our lives we have the privilege of being *led* by God. The Holy Spirit is the very presence of God and resides in the life of every born-again believer in Jesus. So let's look at just a few of the descriptors used for the Holy Spirit.

1. The Holy Spirit is our *Helper*. Consider the runner. Regardless of the distance, this athlete must have the mental focus to continue running even when it becomes difficult. All throughout the race, he/she passes people standing alongside the route. As the runner goes by, the people cheer

and shout words of encouragement. Phrases such as, "Keep going," "You can do it," and "We believe in you!" represent some of the support that can be heard. As the runner nears the finish line, the size of the crowd seems to increase and there is even more encouragement not to stop rather to continue all the way through to the finish line. That is exactly what the role of the Holy Spirit is in the life of a born-again believer. He is our Helper. He consoles us and comforts us in the tough times and moves us to greater works for the kingdom. The world cannot accept Him because they do not see Him or know Him (John 14:16–17), but for the Christian, He is a mighty Helper!

2. The Holy Spirit is our *Teacher* (John 14:26). I have always been amazed at reactions to the Bible. People either dive into it and depend on its truth or they avoid it like the plague. Anytime I hear someone question the authority or dependability of the Bible, I sadly realize that they are speaking without the aid of the Holy Spirit. One of the great hallmarks of the Christian life is cherishing, appreciating, and depending on the Bible and its authority in our lives. Truly this book is the *very* Word of God. It is living and active and able to judge the thoughts and intentions of our hearts (Hebrews 4:12). The Holy Spirit acts as Teacher by opening up the words on the pages of scripture and teaching us truths for us to apply in our daily lives!

3. The Holy Spirit is the *Spirit of Truth* (John 15:26). Jesus did not come to create *a* way to eternal life rather He said, "I *am* the way, the truth, and the life" (John 14:6). Eternal life is defined in scripture as *knowing* God the Father and Jesus Christ whom He has sent (John 17:3). To know Jesus personally is to have the capacity to discern truth from lies. We are able to recognize God's handiwork as well as identify when the enemy is wreaking havoc. The Holy Spirit gives us spiritual eyes to see what the rest of the world is helpless to acknowledge, that Jesus Christ is the King of Kings and Lord of Lords!

4. Finally, the Holy Spirit is our *Advocate* (1 John 2:1). Just like a defense attorney represents a client in a court of law, Jesus sits at the right hand of the Father in heaven and acts as our Advocate. It is because of Jesus that we can approach God's throne of grace with confidence (Hebrew 4:16), knowing that He understands us (Psalm 103:14), and that He has walked in our shoes. He can sympathize with our weaknesses. Because of that, He becomes an effective Advocate when we stray from God's best for our lives (Hebrews 4:15). The Holy Spirit is our guarantee that our sins have been forgiven and that we now belong to God through Jesus Christ!

The Holy Spirit gives us spiritual fuel empowering us to live our lives for God. Spend the rest of your day praising God, celebrating, and living in the power of the Holy Spirit!

Spiritual Fishing

"Follow Me, and I will make you *fishers* of men" (Matthew 4:19).

Today: Read Matthew 4

Let's begin by defining the word "church." Often we think of the church as a *location*. We might say something such as, "I'm *going* to church today." By this, we are usually referring to a worship service or group meeting that is taking place inside a building. Others think of the church as a specific *denomination*. There is absolutely nothing wrong with this type of expression; however, it fails to really define the church. Truthfully, the church is not a location, building, or specific denomination rather it consists of *people*. The church is *all* born-again believers and followers of Jesus Christ worldwide.

Our passage today demonstrates where it all began. Jesus took some ordinary fisherman and extended an invitation for them to leave their profession and to go on an eternal mission with Him. Jesus used language that they could understand by declaring that, figuratively, they would still be fishing, but now the object of their pursuit would be human souls. So what does this mean for us today?

First, we need to acknowledge that *all* authority in heaven and on earth has been given to Jesus Christ (Matthew 28:18). This is the very basis for understanding the mission of the church. This is the *why* behind *what* we do. Jesus *is* Savior. He *is* Lord. He gives the church (all believers) the authority to go "fishing."

Secondly, we need to understand our mission. We are to preach the gospel (the good news) to *all* creation (Mark 16:15). Every person that we come in contact with should have the opportunity to hear that they *can* be saved. When an individual *does* accept this good news and *is* saved, it is our responsibility to guide them toward baptism (their outward testimony that they now belong to Jesus) and to teach them so that they can grow spiritually (Matthew 28:19–20). For the believer, salvation is truly the starting line, not the finish. As Christians, we are in process and the teaching ministry of the church is a vital piece of accomplishing all that God wants for us as we grow up and mature in our walk with Christ.

Lastly, we need to approach people, without judgmental attitudes (Luke 6:37). We should share what Christ has done for them with gentleness and respect (1 Peter 3:15). I think the analogy of fishing is important here. In the twenty-first century world, at least in North America, the idea of fishing is often thought of as using bait and a hook. I believe it would be more helpful if the church would consider the first century fishing model of using nets, rather than hooks. The church is not here to use some kind of bait or lure to attract people. We are not attempting to draw people in so that we can insert the hook!

Another misrepresentation that can arise from the bait and hook analogy is that fishing is often thought of as "man against fish." The sharing of one's faith can then be reduced to "Christian against non-believer." I believe too many people feel that they somehow have to come up with an answer for every objection thrown their way instead of just respectfully speaking truth into people's lives as they have opportunity. This might also be one of the reasons some Christians duck out of sharing their faith with others. I do not believe this accurately describes the sharing of good news.

The mission of the church is more like casting out a net, pulling it into the boat, and then repeating the process. Jesus is the Light of the world, and He has equipped us, giving the church the highest mission on earth, to share the good news with the whole world. So grab your nets and happy fishing!

"I [Jesus] am the Light of the world; he who follows Me will not walk in the darkness, but will have the Light of life" (John 8:12). "You (the church) are the light of the world. Let your light shine before men in such a way that they may see your good works and glorify your Father who is in heaven" (Matthew 5:14,16).

Priorities

Therefore if you are presenting your offering at
the altar, and there remember that your brother
has something against you, leave your offering
there before the altar and go; *first be reconciled*
to your brother, and then come and present your
offering. (Matthew 5:23–24)

Today: Read Matthew 5

Today's passage reveals to us an eternal truth about what God values
most—*reconciliation*. To be reconciled is to bring into agreement or
harmony. It is to restore a relationship with another. The brother in
this passage could be a relative, a fellow Christian, a coworker, or
just an acquaintance. Jesus tells us that this reconciliation is to take
priority over presenting an offering to God. For clarification, let's
put this in the modern church context. Picture a time when we have
attended church. Singing, giving an offering, listening to a sermon,
praying, or any other activity that we have engaged in during the
service can be included in the *giving* of an offering to God. It is all
worship and it is what we are to be doing throughout the entire service. So Jesus is instructing us that in the middle of these activities,
if a person comes to our mind, someone who has something against
us, we should leave what we are doing and go and be reconciled with
that individual.

When I was a pastor, I can recall on one occasion telling the
congregation that if they were faced with this situation to go ahead
and leave, walk out of the service, and go find that individual. Social

construct might suggest that it is rude to walk out of a service, but Jesus not only gives us permission to do this, He instructs us to.

So why is reconciliation so important to God? He is relational and wants to see His creation live in the same harmonious relationship in which the Father, Son, and Spirit exist. I believe broken relationships grieve the heart of God. Whether we are estranged from Him or from one another, the Bible gives us good reason to believe that God cares and that He is willingly to work in any relationship that is open to His intervention. We are reminded that God's love for us is to be reciprocated to others:

In this is love, not that we loved God, but that He loved us and sent His Son to be the propitiation for our sins. Beloved, if God so loved us, *we also ought to love one another* (1 John 4:10-11).

God has taken care of the great divided separating mankind from Himself through the sacrifice of His own Son upon the cross. God's reconciling us to Himself should be the motivation for us to be reconciled to one another. Also, the church has been given the mission of telling others *how* to be reconciled to God (2 Corinthians 5:18-20). It would be hypocritical at best and impossible at worst for the church to carry the message of reconciliation while remaining estranged to one another. So let's end with some practical applications for this passage.

1. We are only responsible for how *we* handle reconciliation. It is quite possible for us to attempt to mend ways with another only for that effort to be met with hostility and rejection. We should be sensitive to God's direction regarding the number of attempts and timing of our efforts. It is possible however that after we have made our effort, that we will have to leave the situation in God's hands.

2. We are *not* responsible for how others respond to our attempt at making peace. Every person will answer for the thoughts, words, and deeds of their life. We need to make sure that we are right with God and that we have done everything possible to live at peace with others. We should

not allow the refusal of another to serve as baggage in our own lives.

3. Finally, be forgiving—*all* of the time (Matthew 18:21–22). If we are the offender, we should go quickly, apologize, and be reconciled with the one that we have offended. However, if the offense was against us, we must forgive! We will find that forgiving freely will set us free from any burden that holding grudges brings. We should forgive as often as is necessary and then let God deal with those who have offended us.

Do nothing from selfishness or empty conceit, but with humility of mind *regard one another as more important than yourselves*; do not merely look out for your own personal interests, but also for the interests of others (Philippians 2:3–4).

Rich toward God

Do not store up for yourselves *treasures on earth*,
where moth and rust destroy, and where thieves
break in and steal. But *store up* for yourselves
treasures in heaven, where neither moth nor rust
destroys, and where thieves do not break in or
steal; for where your treasure is, there your heart
will be also. (Matthew 6:19–21)

Today: Read Matthew 6

Our passage today reminds us of the importance of keeping our
eyes focused on the things of God and not on earthly things. Jesus
tells us *not* to store up treasures on earth rather we are to store
up treasures in heaven. This is foolishness for the unbeliever. For
the Christian, however, this makes perfectly good sense. After all,
material things are only for use in this world but serve absolutely
no purpose beyond this life. As believers, we understand that we
own nothing and that all of our possessions, even our children, are
on loan to us only for a time. Jesus reminds us not to worry about
money (verse 25) but to seek first *His* kingdom and *His* righteousness then all of those other things will be added (verse 33). Here are
some truths for us to consider when assessing our attitude toward
wealth.

Truth Number 1:

> No one can serve two masters; for either he will
> hate the one and love the other, or he will be
> devoted to one and despise the other. You cannot
> serve God and wealth (Matthew 6:24).

We have to make a choice. We cannot serve God and wealth at the same time. Jesus is not saying that it is wrong to make money rather He is reminding us not to *serve* money. When our goal in life is to see how much we can acquire, we start down the road of serving money. We have to make a choice. We are either living for God or we are living for ourselves. It's that simple.

Truth Number 2:

> "Beware and be on your guard against every
> form of greed; for not even when one has an
> abundance does his life consist of his possessions"
> (Luke 12:15).

Our possessions define *what* we have, not *who* we are. Jesus reminds us to guard our hearts against any form of greed. He illustrates this point by telling a parable of a man who was extremely wealthy. This man had acquired so much that his barns could not contain all that he had. So he decided to build bigger barns to support his wealth. In Jesus's day, the hearers lived in an agrarian society, so crops equaled wealth for them. Today, we can think of this as someone who works hard his/her whole life and has amassed wealth. This can take the form of bank accounts, investments, property, and so forth. Listen to what the man tells himself, "Soul, you have many goods laid up for many years to come; take your ease, eat, drink and be merry" (Luke 12:19). God responds to the man by saying, "You fool! This very night your soul is required of you; and now who will own what you have prepared?" (verse 20) So is the man who stores up treasure for himself but is not rich toward God (verse 21). The problem was not the man's wealth rather it was his outlook on life believing (falsely) that his abundance was in his possessions. He was materially wealthy but poor in spiritual things.

Truth Number 3:

> "Truly I say to you, it is hard for a rich man to enter the kingdom of heaven. Again I say to you, it is easier for a camel to go through the eye of a needle, than for a rich man to enter the kingdom of God" (Matthew 19:23–24).

Money can actually act as a barrier between a man and God. Jesus reminded His disciples of how difficult it is for a rich man to enter the kingdom of heaven. Is it possible for a person to have material wealth *and* be a Christian? Of course! But for the believer, money is not the goal of life rather his/her wealth merely acts as a means of blessing others.

As believers, we are heirs to the kingdom of God. Everything that is His belongs to us as well. This godly wealth is eternal. Believers never have to worry about *not* having their needs met. When we seek God first, He provides everything else that we need to live an abundant life in Jesus. I hope today finds you rich toward God. Take some time to praise Him for your wealth, materially and spiritually!

> "For what is a man profited if he gains the whole world, and loses or forfeits himself?" (Luke 9:25).

Better Than Any Earthly Parent

"If you then, being evil, know how to give good gifts to your children, *how much more* will your Father who is in heaven give what is good to those who ask Him" (Matthew 7:11).

Today: Read Matthew 7

What a privilege it is to talk to God about everything. In today's passage, Jesus is instructing us to ask, to seek, and to knock (verse 7). The tense of the verbs used in this passage refer to a continual action, so we can translate the verse "*keep* asking," "*keep* seeking," and "*keep* knocking." The principle behind this instruction is given to us in the very next verse. *Everyone* who asks receives, whoever seeks *will* find, and whoever knocks, the door *will* be opened (verse 8). This biblical principle informs us of the certainty of God's response.

But our focus today is on the remainder of the passage. God's character and nature are on display as Jesus teaches us *why* this principle exists. Jesus uses two examples of earthly parenting in which anyone can relate. These two examples are stated in the form of a question. "If your child asks you for something beneficial (bread), you as the parent would not give them something harmful or useless (stone) would you?" (verse 9). Jesus follows with a second illustration. "If your child comes to you and again asks for something beneficial (fish), you would not give them something harmful or unhelpful like a snake would you?" (verse 10). Of course, the answer is that no good parent would do such a thing. So now the character of God is compared to the earthly parenting examples. "If you then being evil, know how to give good gifts to your children, how much more..." (verse 11). It's a comparative statement. Even fallen mankind has the God-given ability to nurture and care for their young. So Jesus says, *How much more* will your Father who is in heaven give what is good to those who ask." It's not even close. God is better at caring for us than we are at caring for ourselves.

God will give us what is *good*. The word "good" can be defined as that which is useful, pleasant, agreeable, joyful, and happy. This goodness is salutary, favorable in promoting health, and conducive to some beneficial purpose. And to whom is God going to give these good things? He gives them to those who ask! Now, the principle that "everyone who asks will receive" makes sense. God is a better giver than any earthly parent and is willing to gift us with things that are beneficial and promote our spiritual growth and well-being.

But there is still one more thing. The very next verse is often called the golden rule and it reads like this:

> "In everything, therefore, treat people the same
> way you want them to treat you, for this is the
> Law and the Prophets" (Matthew 7:12).

Some translations treat this verse as a separate thought, apart from the passages on asking, but the text supports the idea that the golden rule flows from the very character and nature of God (some translations us *therefore*, others *so*). So because God is a loving, heavenly Father, ready to pour good things into the life of the one who asks, we are *therefore* to treat other people the way we want them to treat us. By treating others this way, we are fulfilling the Law and the Prophets. I believe the church has two very important obligations to the world.

1. We should proclaim the truth found in today's passage, namely that God is a loving heavenly Father.
2. We are to display this truth by the way we treat others. This positive, loving treatment of others only validates our

proclamation to the wonderfulness of God. Failure to do so only confuses and causes skepticism on the part of those seeking truth. Keep asking, keep seeking, and keep knocking! God truly is better than any earthly parent!

The Power of Faith

"Truly I say to you, I have not found such great *faith* with anyone in Israel. Go, it shall be done for you as you have *believed*." (Matthew 8:10,13).

Today: Read Matthew 8

The Bible is full of "main things." These are the things that appear repeatedly throughout scripture. For the one who makes a point to spend time in God's Word every day, these truths are hard to miss. Throughout the gospels, we see the power of faith on display as Jesus heals and delivers people from sin and brokenness. Today's passage is one such event.

A Roman centurion makes a plea on behalf of his servant. This servant was reported to be at the centurion's home, lying paralyzed, and "fearfully tormented" (verse 6). Jesus agrees to come to the man's home and heal the servant. But upon hearing this, the centurion admits his own unworthiness and implores Jesus not to come rather just to "say the word" for his servant to be healed. This man recognized the authority and power that Jesus has over sin, sickness, and everything else that plagues mankind. Jesus recognized the man's faith and healed the servant instantly. Don't miss Jesus's words as He says, "Go, it shall be done for you *as you have believed*" (verse 13). Jesus acted on the man's faith, thus what the man *believed* became reality in his life.

This certainly is not the only place in scripture in which we see Jesus act in response to faith. Jesus responds to a sinful woman by declaring her sins forgiven (Luke 7:48). Again, don't miss Jesus's words, "Your *faith* has saved you, go in peace" (Luke 7:50). Jesus identifies the woman's faith and it acts as the conduit through which God's forgiveness and healing flowed. Jesus healed a woman who had a longstanding medical issue and declared that, "Her *faith* had made her well" (Matthew 9:22). Jesus even responds to the faith of others. When the friends of a paralytic bring him to Jesus, He recognizes *their* faith saying, "Take courage, son, your sins are forgiven" (Matthew 9:2). And on top of that, Jesus heals him and the man got up and walked home (Matthew 9:7). So while faith is the means by which the power of God is displayed, a lack of faith can also hinder God's working in our lives.

In the same chapter that we are reading today, the disciples are in a boat with Jesus. The peaceful day gives way to a great storm, which sends the disciples into a life or death panic. "Save us Lord, we are perishing!" was the cry of Jesus's followers (Matthew 8:25). His reply to them is telling, "Why are you afraid, you men of *little faith*?" (verse 26) Likewise, when the disciples were faced with an attempt to cast out a demon from a demon-possessed man, they were unsuccessful. They inquired as to why they could not accomplish the task. Jesus responded by saying, "Because of the *littleness of your faith*" (Matthew 17:20). Jesus goes on to teach us that if we have faith, even the size of a mustard seed, we can move mountains and nothing will be impossible for us (Matthew 17:20).

Faith is the key that unlocks the door to the power of God in our lives. It is how we are saved (Acts 16:31). It is the difference between forgiveness and condemnation (John 3:18). And without it, we *cannot* please God (Hebrews 11:6). Trust Him today and watch the power of God displayed in your life!

What the World Needs Now

"Seeing the people, He felt *compassion* for them because they were distressed and dispirited like sheep without a shepherd" (Matthew 9:36).

Today: Read Matthew 9

People are hurting in the world today. People are confused and fearful about the future. People are suffering from addictions, broken relationships, and all kinds of physical ailments. Sometimes people dig themselves into predicaments that they are helpless to solve. And as with someone who has fallen into a hole, when people have hit rock bottom, they do not need a shovel, they need a hand. This is where the church should stand at the ready. Today's passage comes from the very end of the chapter and perfectly illustrates an action plan for every believer to positively impact society by emulating Christ.

"Jesus was going through all the cities and villages, teaching in their synagogues and proclaiming the gospel of the kingdom and healing every kind of disease and every kind of sickness" (Matthew 9:35).

First, notice that Jesus was *going*. He was not sitting in one location waiting for people to come to Him (although they did). He was in motion, traveling through all of the cities and villages. As Jesus traveled, He was engaged in three activities: teaching, proclaiming, and healing.

Teaching in the synagogues is the equivalent of having Bible study groups today. Unless the church is prepared to teach people, growth cannot and will not take place. Just like physically working out, spiritual fitness does not just happen. It takes desire, dedication, and diligence. Neglecting Bible study only leads to spiritual atrophy.

In addition to teaching, the church should be *proclaiming* good news. The gospel *is* good news and it is for the world. Redemption *is* possible and the church is responsible for preaching this message to *all* of creation (Mark 16:15).

Often the church is thought of as only dealing with spiritual matters but we are all made in the image of God (Genesis 1:26–27) and as such, we are individuals with different facets to our existence. Taking care of our minds and bodies is equally as important as spiritual matters. The church can pray for the healing of an individual but should also assist the people in being proactive with their health by making the connection between physical and spiritual well-being. Training people to work out their minds and bodies can greatly reduce the possibility of depression and physical disease. So Jesus went about teaching, proclaiming, and healing and we should be doing the same.

> "Seeing the people, He felt *compassion* for them,
> because they were distressed and dispirited like
> sheep without a shepherd" (Matthew 9:36).

Of course, the church will only engage in these actions when they authentically have *compassion* for others. When Jesus saw that the people were distressed and dispirited, He did not scold them, tell them where they had gone wrong, or chastised them (He reserved that for the religious folks). Jesus met the people's deepest needs *because* he felt compassion for them. I find it truly amazing that God acted on our behalf by sending Jesus rather than leaving us without hope. Because God is love, we should demonstrate love (1 John 4:10–11). Because God is merciful, we should show mercy (Luke 6:36). And because God cares for the world, so should we (John 3:16–17).

"Then He said to His disciples, 'The harvest
is plentiful, but the workers are *few*'"
(Matthew 9:37).

So this verse, although true, should perplex us. "The harvest is plentiful, but the workers are few" simply means that God desires to do a great work in the world yet there are few believers that are willing to go and proclaim the good news. We have been saved from all of our sin, blessed with all of the riches of God's blessings, declared heirs to God's kingdom, and given eternal life through the Holy Spirit. Yet in spite of it all, we often fail to tell other people that *they* can be saved as well. This is not a guilt trip, simply an opportunity for us to ask ourselves, "Are we doing what God has called us to do in expanding His kingdom to a hurting, distressed, and dispirited world?" I think it is a fair question.

"Therefore beseech the Lord of the harvest to *send
out* workers into His harvest" (Matthew 9:38).

Finally, while evaluating our own participation in kingdom work, the church is to pray for God to convict believers to step out of their comfort zones and follow Him by faith. Are you fulfilling your God-given purpose? Are you willing to step out in faith?

Incompatibility

Brother will betray brother to death, and a father his child; and children will rise up against parents and cause them to be put to death. You will be hated by all *because of My name*, but it is the one who has endured to the end who will be saved. (Matthew 10:21–22)

Today: Read Matthew 10

Sometimes living the Christian life can be difficult. Our passage today, which is outlined throughout the entire chapter, deals with the complexity of placing Christ as priority in our lives. When we refer to Jesus as the Prince of Peace, we are referring to the reality that His sacrificial death makes a way for mankind to enjoy peace with God. It does not, however, mean that there will be peace between a Christian and everyone else in the world. In fact, it is quite the opposite. Next to physical persecution, I believe one of the most difficult situations that a believer can face is the divide between family members over the name of Jesus. Believers who have unsaved family members will often experience hardship simply because light and darkness are entirely incompatible. In order to navigate this portion of the Christian life, let's look at six components to Jesus's teaching.

1. Don't Be Surprised At Persecution

A disciple is not above his teacher, nor a slave above his master. It is enough for the disciple that he become like his teacher, and the slave like his master. If they have called the head of the house Beelzebub, how much more will they malign the members of his household (Matthew 10:24–25).

Jesus reminds us that as He walked the earth, mankind rejected Him. As a follower of Christ, we can expect the same kind of persecution in our lives. It is amazing to ponder that the Creator of the universe, the One who gives us the very breath in our lungs, took on human flesh, came down from heaven, and walked among His creation. But because of the evil that resides in the human heart, Jesus was not greeted with open arms rather He was persecuted by the very people whom He created. "A disciple is not above his teacher" simply means that if Jesus was received this way, we should not be surprised when we are treated likewise.

2. Understanding Incompatibility

"For from now on, five members in one household will be divided, three against two and two against three. They will be divided, father against son and son against father, mother against daughter and daughter against mother, mother-in-law against daughter-in-law and daughter-in-law against mother-in-law" (Luke 12:52–53)

The Bible does not hide the reality that believers and non-believers within the same family will often be at odds over the name of Jesus. If we come from a family that honors and serves the Lord then we are truly blessed. To have blood relatives that also share our spiritual DNA is a gift from God. But for those of us who are a part of an unbelieving family, life can be difficult and persecution (in some form) is almost sure to come. Even in "civil" families, beneath all of the small talk and pleasantries, there is a division of the heart. We need to understand the reason for this incompatibility. When someone is born again, they receive the Holy Spirit and consequently are given a new outlook on life and eternity. Those without the Spirit cannot understand why someone who "used to be fun" would now desire to put God first in their life. This life is foolishness to the unbeliever. One is forgiven and redeemed, the other lost and spiritually dead. These individuals are on two completely different roads. This creates the incompatibility. So Jesus gives us some advice for overcoming.

3. Be Intelligent

> "Behold, I send you out as sheep in the midst of wolves; so be shrewd as serpents and innocent as doves" (Matthew 10:16).

It is perfectly fine for a believer in Jesus to be shrewd. Not only are we given permission, we are *told* to be astute in spiritual matters. The key is to couple that with "being as innocent as doves." A believer is to use his/her discernment for the purposes of growing the kingdom. Living by the Spirit of God means having the ability to discern a situation and then acting appropriately. Knowing when to speak and when to be silent are a part of being shrewd. Be ever discerning when handling those who are outside of the body of Christ.

4. Do Not Fear Mankind

> Therefore do not fear them, for there is nothing concealed that will not be revealed or hidden that will not be known. Do not fear those who kill the body but are unable to kill the soul; but rather fear Him who is able to destroy both soul and body in hell. So do not fear; you are more valuable than many sparrows. (Matthew 10:26, 28, 31)

Three times, in this passage, Jesus tells us *not* to fear mankind. Every effort made against the kingdom of God will ultimately fail. The Bible tells us that those who hate Jesus do not come into the Light for fear that their deeds will be exposed (John 3:20). Jesus reminds us that *everything* will be revealed in time. This includes our actions, what we think, and what we do in secret as well as our motives. Practically, we are not to fear man because they can only affect our lives here on earth but are powerless to disturb what we have eternally. So Christians, do not fear, we are valuable to God.

5.   Be Faithful To God

> "Therefore everyone who confesses Me before men, I will also confess him before My Father who is in heaven. But whoever denies Me before men, I will also deny him before My Father who is in heaven" (Matthew 10:32–33).

When faced with the opportunity to shy away from our faith and fold to the pressures of the world, remember these words, "Everyone who confesses Jesus before others, Jesus will confess them before God in heaven." Do not be ashamed of Christ or the gospel. When others scoff at us for being a follower of Jesus, stand firm. Our public acknowledgement of Christ is a testimony that God is indeed with us and that we belong to Him (1 John 4:15).

6.   You Have To Make A Choice

> He who loves father or mother more than Me is not worthy of Me; and he who loves son or daughter more than Me is not worthy of Me. And he who does not take his cross and follow after Me is not worthy of Me. He who has found his life will lose it, and he who has lost his life for My sake will find it. (Matthew 10:37–39)

Finally, you have to make a choice. Walking with God is the most rewarding thing you will ever do but it does require sacrifice. Jesus does not hide the fact that He *must* become the most important person in our lives. He is to be at the center of our existence. We should love our spouse but not put them in the *place* of Christ.

We are to love and honor our parents but not *more* than Christ. We should love and cherish our children but not *above* Christ. I find that in the attempt to love our families there can be a danger in placing them above our relationship with Jesus. When this happens, it really is nothing short of idolatry. But the reality is this, when we put Jesus first, our relationships improve. We are able to be better sons and daughters. We become more loving to our spouse and highly effective as parents.

I do not believe that it is a coincidence that Jesus spent so much time talking about this area of life. It is difficult to see the people we love live without God in their lives. To consider that they are living without salvation and apart from the will of God can be a heavy burden to bear. But be patient, persistent, and prayerful! Honor God with your life, knowing that He *will* use you to make an eternal impact on others!

Tired and Burdened?

Come to Me, all who are weary and heavy-laden, and *I will give you rest*. Take My yoke upon you and learn from Me, for I am gentle and humble in heart, and *you will find rest for your souls*. For My yoke is easy and My burden is light. (Matthew 11:28–30)

Today: Read Matthew 11

Living in this world can sometimes be difficult. Life can wear us down and discourage us. But the church is to act as a sanctuary, a place where one can find forgiveness and redemption. The church is a physical representation of heaven on earth and a place where love, joy, and peace are to be experienced and enjoyed. Jesus invites *all* who are weary and burdened to *come* to Him. This invitation is echoed throughout scripture. "If anyone is thirsty, let him *come* to Me and drink" (John 7:37). "And let the one who is thirsty *come*, let the one who wishes *take* the water of life without cost" (Revelation 22:17). This invitation to "come" is confirmed by the Holy Spirit and the church is to act as the conduit through which it is transmitted. This invitation goes out to *all* who are weary and burdened.

To be weary is self-explanatory. We have all had times in our lives when we are physically, mentally, emotionally, and spiritually drained. These are times when we need a fresh encounter with God. Similarly, to be burdened is to have a load placed upon us. Burdens come in all shapes and sizes and can be placed on us by others or even ourselves. You might find it interesting that the word used in today's passage includes burdens dealing with religious rites and unwarranted precepts. In other words, the burden can come from *religion*. This was a problem in the first century church. We learn that there were some who continued to direct people to observe the Law of Moses as a part of salvation (Acts 15:5). The people were placing religious burdens on others that they were not even able to keep themselves (Acts 15:9–10). Jesus spoke against this type of religious oppression by saying, "Woe to you lawyers, for you weigh men down with burdens hard to bear, while you yourselves will not even touch the burdens with one of your fingers" (Luke 11:46). We are also warned, once set free in Jesus, not to allow anyone to weigh us down with religious burdens rather we are to stand firm in our faith and not be placed again under a yoke of slavery (Galatians 5:1).

The promise for all who come to Jesus is that He will give them rest, *spiritual* rest. To rest is to ease, relieve, and refresh our souls. The word "rest" literally means to create an *intermission*. We could all use a respite from time to time. If we are not in the habit of carving out some time in our day to focus on God through prayer and the study of His Word, I want to encourage everyone to make that a priority. This book is designed to assist us in that endeavor. So the invitation is to *come* to Jesus and receive *rest*.

But that is not all. Jesus also invites us to take on His *yoke* (as opposed to religious yokes) and to *learn* from Him. Rest comes when we fully understand who God is and how He has revealed Himself to us through His Son Jesus (Hebrews 1:2). One of my favorite pictures of Christ is His washing the feet of the disciples as an example of how we are to treat those around us (John 13:14–17). I want us to take that in for a moment. The Creator of the universe, the One and only all-powerful God, took on human flesh, and was kneeling to wash the feet of those He created. I believe that is what Jesus means to take *His* yoke and to learn from *Him*. He *is* gentle and humble in heart. Jesus tells us that taking on His yoke and learning from Him *will* result in our finding rest for our souls. Humanity longs to know that they are loved and that there is hope for them in the future. Jesus embodies the good news. God *is* love and there *is* hope for all who come to Jesus, take on His yoke, and learn from Him.

Finally, Jesus describes why *rest* is the natural by-product for those who trust Him. Rather than embedding ourselves in religious activity, Jesus describes *His* yoke as easy and light. The word "easy" can be translated "pleasurable." It means useful, pleasant, and kind (as opposed to harsh, hard, and bitter). This is the same word translated "kindness" in the fruit of the Spirit (Galatians 5:22–23). It is also used in our instruction to be *kind* to one another (Ephesians 4:32). Jesus's yoke is pleasurable, kind, and easy. It is *not* harsh, hard, or bitter. Jesus's yoke is light and will not weigh us down. Jesus paints a picture quite the opposite of what much of religion offers, in which God is portrayed as a harsh taskmaster, waiting for His subjects to falter and be punished.

So if you are tired, confused, desperate, restless, depressed, or burdened, *come* to Jesus. Trade in your religious burdens and rituals for an authentic, genuine relationship with the God who loves you more than you could ever know. Take on the yoke of Christ and learn from Him. This world can be harsh. Religious yokes merely add to what is already a difficult road to navigate. Come to Jesus and He *will* give you rest!

Now to the one who works (for his salvation), his wage is not credited as a favor, but as what is due. But to the one who does not work but believes (trusts) in Him (Jesus) who justifies the ungodly, his *faith* is credited as righteousness (Romans 4:4–5).

What God Desires

"But if you had known what this means, '*I desire compassion and not a sacrifice*,' you would not have condemned the innocent" (Matthew 12:7)

Today: Read Matthew 12

When Jesus walked the earth, there seemed to be two consistently different reactions toward Him. For those who were living in sin, oppressed, suffering, in anguish, and in the grip of the enemy, to see Jesus was a reason to *celebrate* and *rejoice*. Jesus brought with Him real hope of victory, healing, and spiritual freedom. Jesus came to save, redeem, and restore lives. Contrast that to the legalistic, rule-obsessed Pharisees. They were "representatives" of God yet did not even recognize Jesus or His glory, even when displayed right in front of them. Today's passage is a good primer on what God desires in the life of every born-again believer in Jesus Christ, and its foundation is in Jesus's words, "I desire compassion, and not sacrifice." Everything that we claim to believe and profess should move from mere knowledge to a demonstration of who God is by pouring these five characteristics into the lives of others.

1. Be Loving

Love is the first descriptor used in defining the fruit of God's Spirit (Galatians 5:22–23). I do not believe that this is a coincidence. Arguably, all of the other traits of the Christian life are dependent on how loving we are. All that God has done for us stems from *His* love.

Therefore, our treatment and handling of others can be assessed by how much we *love* them. Love demonstrates that we *know* God (1 John 4:7–8). Our words, beliefs, and sacrificial actions, void of love, become useless and unprofitable (1 Corinthians 13:1–3). Love is the fulfillment of the Law of God (Romans 13:10). Jesus is the embodiment of the love of God but, in today's passage, the Pharisees were more concerned about the statute regarding the Sabbath than they were of Jesus and the disciples. They completely missed the glory of God.

2.   Be Forgiving

It seems that everyone wants to be forgiven but not everyone is willing *to* forgive. When it comes to *our* sin and failure, we want God "to cast it as far as the east is from the west" (Psalm 103:12) while retaining the bitterness and anger associated with being wronged by others. In the Lord's Prayer, we find a phrase that goes like this, "And forgive us our debts, as we also have forgiven our debtors" (Matthew 6:12). Have you ever prayed that before? When we pray that to God, we are asking Him to forgive us in direct proportion to our releasing others from their debts against us. Jesus elaborates on this truth by instructing us that if we forgive others, God *will* forgive us. However, if we are unwilling to forgive, then God will *not* forgive us of our sins (Matthew 6:14–15). We should be a gracious people, ready to forgive as many times as is necessary (Matthew 18:21–22).

3.   Be Merciful

The issue of forgiveness is not the only place in scripture in which we find this idea of proportional response from God. Consider the following:

> Be merciful, just as your Father is merciful. Do not judge, and you will not be judged; and do not condemn, and you will not be condemned; pardon, and you will be pardoned. Give, and

it will be given to you. For by your standard of
measure it will be measured to you in return.
(Luke 6:36–38)

We are to display mercy in the lives of others. This means that
we withhold any penalty that we feel is due another for an offense
against us. Jesus tells us that we are not judged *when* we do not judge
others. We will not be condemned *when* we refuse to condemn. We
will be pardoned for our offenses *as* we pardon others as well. "Give
to others and it *will* be given to you as well." Do you see the recipro-
cal pattern in this passage? "By the same standard of measure it will
be measured to us in return."

4.   Be Humble

Christians should be in state of constant thankfulness for the
salvation, grace, and mercy of God in their own lives. We have *all*
sinned and fallen short of God's glory (Romans 3:23) and when we
break even one of God's laws, we become guilty of the *whole* thing
(James 2:10). Remembering these truths should keep us not only in a
state of thankfulness but humility as well. Jesus humbled Himself to
become the propitiation for the sins of the world (Philippians 2:6–7)
therefore we are to have this same humility in ourselves. This means
that our lives are not just about *our* wants and *our* desires. Believers
should be marked with a characteristic of regarding others as *more*
important than themselves as well as looking out for the interests of
others (Philippians 2:3–4).

5.   Be Compassionate

Compassion is characterized by mercy, kindness, and goodwill. It is the ability to sympathize with the plight of another human
being. This kind of compassion is accompanied by a desire to help
them. Lacking compassion, the Pharisees "condemned the innocent"
by focusing on the Law rather than on their fellow man. Christians

should share in displaying the same kind of compassion that Jesus demonstrated throughout His earthly ministry.

I believe the key to understanding these truths is found in the verse preceding our passage, "But I say to you that something *greater* than the temple is here" (verse 6). Jesus *is* greater indeed. The Pharisees lacked compassion in part because they believed that the letter of the Law was the process by which God would bless mankind. They failed to see that someone greater had come on the scene, thus they missed the very God that they believed they were serving. Only when we exhibit these characteristics in abundance can we really make claim to be living "godly" lives and being "Christ-like." Keeping these things in mind will also assist in guarding the church against becoming merely people who "know a lot but don't show a lot."

Unbelief in Your Own Backyard

> He came to His hometown and began teaching them in their synagogue. And they took offense at Him. But Jesus said to them, "A prophet is not without honor *except* in his hometown and in his own household." And He did not do many miracles there because of their unbelief. (Matthew 13:54,57–58)

Today: Read Matthew 13

This chapter is full of wonderful parables used by Jesus to explain the kingdom of heaven. But it is the last passage that we will focus on today. Jesus returns to His hometown and begins to teach in the synagogue, a practice that He had consistently followed as He traveled from town to town. The people marveled at His wisdom and miraculous powers. However, this scene does not end like we might think. I believe there are three important items for us to consider.

First, scripture tells us that the people in Jesus's hometown "took offense at Him." To take offense is literally "to be snared by someone or something." It means that the person acts as a *stumbling block*. It is to distrust someone and to see in another what we disapprove of and what hinders us from acknowledging his/her authority. Jesus is a stumbling block for anyone who is attempting to be right with God through works rather than faith. This was the problem that the first century Jews had (Romans 9:32). For some of the people of Israel, it was unfathomable to accept the fact that God had expanded salvation to the Gentiles (the rest of the world). I suppose there are multiple reasons why people take offense at Jesus but the Bible talks much about how righteousness through faith rubs against the self-sufficiency and pride of humanity.

Secondly, Jesus makes a remarkable statement, "A prophet is not without honor, *except* in his hometown and in his own household." Have you ever noticed that it is often much easier to reach strangers with the gospel than it is to reach your own family members? Those that are closest to us know us better than the rest of the world. Our family knows who we really are. This intimate knowledge can sometimes act as a barrier to reaching our relatives because they expect (sometimes unfairly) for us, as believers, to behave better than we often do. Take for example the pastor who preaches a sermon on patience, only to yell at his family the very same afternoon. Jesus had no flaws but perhaps the familiarity the people of Nazareth had with Him caused them to miss His real identity of being the Son of God.

Lastly, we are told that Jesus did not perform many miracles because of the *unbelief* of the people. By taking offense at Jesus, the people put their unbelief on display. It is impossible to trust (to believe) Jesus and at the same time take offense at Him. We will find ourselves on one side of the fence or the other. Unbelief is identified as the cause of Jesus' lack of miracles in Nazareth. We are given many examples in scripture of Jesus connecting healing and restoration with *faith*. We are told that *all* things are possible to him who *believes* (Mark 9:23).

I hope today finds you trusting in Jesus. Whether or not your family joins you in praising God, keep praying for those closest to you and continue to be faithful to the One who has called you into service. May you find God doing far more in your life than you could have ever thought or imagined (Ephesians 3:20).

Asking with Faith

Peter said to Him, "Lord, if it is You, command me to come to You on the water." And He said, "Come!" And Peter got out of the boat and walked on the water and came toward Jesus. But seeing the wind, he became frightened, and beginning to sink, he cried out, "Lord, save me!" Immediately Jesus stretched out His hand and took hold of him, and said to him, *"You of little faith, why did you doubt?"* When they got into the boat, the wind stopped. And those who were in the boat worshiped Him, saying, "You are certainly God's Son!" (Matthew 14:28–33)

Today: Read Matthew 14

Today we will look at what I consider two of the most important principles for believers who desire to experience fullness in the Christian life.

Principle Number 1: Be bold in asking!

The Bible instructs us to "Be anxious about nothing and pray about everything, letting our requests be made known to God" (Philippians 4:6). Jesus teaches us to be continually asking and assures us that *everyone* who asks receives (Matthew 7:7–8). In our passage today, we see Jesus walking on the water. At first, the disciples are frightened, and why wouldn't they be. A man walking on water isn't exactly the norm for life as we know it. Peter, still questioning whether or not it is Jesus, makes a bold request, "Lord, if it is You, command me to come to You on the water." And Jesus said, "Come!"

Consider what is being asked of Christ. Peter wants to do the same thing that Jesus Himself was doing, and He was perfectly willing to include him in the activity. I love that about God! The Bible tells us that sometimes God may not answer us because we are asking for selfish reasons (James 4:3), but scripture also informs us that we can live in want simply because we do *not* ask (James 4:2). If Peter had never asked, he probably would have never walked on the water. But He did walk on water because he asked! Be bold in your asking. Even if you think that God does not care about a particular issue in your life or feel that He would never answer, ask anyway, and ask boldly!

Principle Number 2: Ask with faith, eliminating any doubt!

This is an incredibly important aspect of our prayer life. Our faith will usually not be tested in answering the question, "*Can* God answer this prayer?" To my knowledge, I have never met a Christian that believes God is limited in His power or ability to answer us. Our faith will usually be tested in answering the question, "*Will* God answer this prayer?" We know He *can* but do we believe that He *will*? This is the true test of faith. Consider the following:

> "But if any of you lacks wisdom, let him ask of God, who gives to all generously and without reproach, and it will be given to him. *But he must ask in faith without any doubting*" (James 1:5–6a).

God gives generously to all without reproach. This means that God is pleased to give to those who ask and He does not find fault or blame in our asking, for He knows what we need even before we ask (Matthew 6:8). But we must ask in *faith*! This is a major principle in understanding how God distributes wisdom or anything else for which we might ask. Doubt must be left out of this process. Consider the following description of those that doubt:

> "For the one who *doubts* is like the surf of the sea, driven and tossed by the wind. For that man *ought not to expect that he will receive anything from the Lord*, being a double-minded man, unstable in all his ways" (James 1:6b–8).

Faith is the currency we use in bringing our requests to our heavenly Father. The one who doubts is described as double-minded (literally two-souled) and unstable individual. In addition, the Bible states that this person should *not* expect to receive anything from the Lord. Faith is the key! This concept is illustrated all throughout the gospels. For the centurion, Jesus says, "Go, it shall be done for you *as you have believed*." And his servant *was* healed at that very moment (Matthew 8:13). For the woman with a hemorrhage, Jesus says, "Daughter, take courage; *your faith has made you well*." At once the woman *was* made well (Matthew 9:22). For the blind men, Jesus says, "It shall be done to you *according to your faith*." And their eyes *were* opened (Matthew 9:29–30). In each instance, Jesus acted on their behalf and indicated that the result was in accordance with their faith.

So let's conclude with our friend Peter. Upon Peter's request to walk on the water, Jesus said, "Come!" For a moment Peter was doing great. Then he saw what was really happening around him and begin to sink and Jesus rescued him. Then Jesus identifies the root of Peter's problem, "You of *little faith*, why did you *doubt*?" Do you see what is happening here? Peter's request was bold and daring. Jesus's response was one of willingness to allow Peter his request. The request was birthed into reality and Peter defied the laws of physics. However, distraction led to a waning of Peter's faith and gave rise to his doubt. And what was the result? He began to sink.

As Christians, we are sons and daughters of God. We are heirs to His kingdom. Our requests should reflect those realities. Consider exercising these two principles in your life this week. Be bold in your asking, eliminate any doubt, and by all means, ask with faith!

> Truly I say to you, whoever says to this mountain, "Be taken up and cast into the sea," and does not doubt in his heart but believes that what he says is going to happen, it will be granted to him. Therefore I say to you, all things for which you pray and ask, believe that you have received them, and they will be granted to you. (Mark 11:23–24)

Spiritual Lip Service

"This people honors Me with their lips, but their heart is far away from Me. But in vain do they worship Me, teaching as doctrines the precepts of men" (Matthew 15:8–9).

Today: Read Matthew 15

Today we find Jesus again dealing with the Pharisees and their obsession with religious rituals. The disciples had failed to ceremonially wash their hands before eating. We wash our hands for sanitary reasons however the Pharisees believed it must be done as a way of pleasing God. Jesus deals with them and eventually announces to the disciples that the Pharisees' concern was unfounded and that eating with unwashed hands does *not* defile them in any way (Matthew 15:20). While dealing with this situation, Jesus quotes from the prophet Isaiah:

> "Because this people draw near with their words and honor Me with their lip service, but they remove their hearts far from Me, and their reverence for Me consists of tradition learned by rote" (Isaiah 29:13).

Jesus is declaring that the Pharisees were fulfilling this prophecy by their attitude and actions. Christ stated that these religious men were claiming worship of God, but He saw through their efforts, knowing that their hearts did *not* reflect an attitude of worship. So what do we need to learn from this passage? I believe we need to guard ourselves from becoming people who outwardly profess worship while lacking true devotion in our hearts. Here are five suggestions to consider when assessing our own worship.

1. Worship is an attitude of the heart.

When you hear the word "worship" what is it that comes to your mind? If you were raised in a Christian home, you might think of worship as the singing portion of a church service. Certainly singing is a part of worship but it encompasses a great deal more. Worship is an attitude that someone has *toward* God, and it begins in the heart. While addressing the Pharisees, Jesus identified that their problem was that outwardly they professed devotion to God while inwardly, they were lacking and misguided. Worship that is pleasing to God begins and flows from our hearts.

2. No one can accurately assess authentic worship other than God and the participant.

Worship is a private matter. There is no single way to worship God therefore everyone is responsible for determining whether or not their heart is genuine. Since God is the object of our worship, He is the ultimate judge in all matters concerning this issue. When we make judgments on the worship of others, we are putting ourselves in the place of God and professing abilities beyond ourselves, namely, the capacity to see into the heart of another. All such judgments are inconsistent with the Christian life.

3. Worship is not limited to any specific genre or style of music.

Music plays an important role in the worship life of many believers. There are numerous options in choosing worship music and most people have their favorites. Generational and geographical factors drive diversity in music. If we could time travel, we would discover that fifteenth century worship music would sound completely different from that of the nineteenth, twentieth, or twenty-first centuries. Likewise, if we were to worship with Christians in Africa, the music would be very different than that of churches in South America, Europe, or Asia. These two factors affect our preference in music. Just keep in mind that whatever you sing to God, sing it with all of your heart!

4. Worship is not limited to a specific location.

You do not have to "be in church" in order to worship God. Worship can happen anywhere at any time. I have a confession to make. My most rewarding times of worship are when I am alone with God. That is not to diminish the importance of corporate worship, just a reminder that worshiping God should be a lifestyle, not just a weekly event. We can praise God every moment of every day. Worship brings glory to God but it also pays dividends for us as well. If praising God is not currently a part of your daily routine, give it a try!

5. Worship comes from hearing the truth and celebrating its reality in your life.

The gospel is good news. When we understand what Jesus has accomplished on the cross and receive His forgiveness and redemption, authentic worship can then flow from a heart of gratitude. Spirit-filled worship is God-pleasing worship. An absence of spiritual freedom can hinder our efforts in offering up praise to God. But when we live in the forgiveness and freedom that comes from embracing the gospel, worship becomes a natural by-product of our lives. The Pharisees, distracted by rules and regulations, were engaging in spiritual lip service. Their outward actions appeared impressive but their hearts gave them away.

Is your life void of worship? If so, what obstacles are keeping you from enjoying this part of the Christian life? Has worship become mundane and ritualistic? Let's be a people that rediscover the joy of authentic worship in our daily lives and then encourage those around us to do the same!

"God is spirit, and those who worship Him must worship in spirit and truth" (John 4:24).

Following Jesus

Then Jesus said to His disciples, "If anyone wishes to come after Me, he must deny himself, and take up his cross and follow Me. For whoever wishes to save his life will lose it; but whoever loses his life for My sake will find it. For what will it profit a man if he gains the whole world and forfeits his soul? Or what will a man give in exchange for his soul? (Matthew 16:24–26)

Today: Read Matthew 16

Today's passage reminds us that following Jesus can be costly. Never forget that salvation is by grace through faith in Jesus's provision on the cross (John 3:18, Galatians 2:16, Acts 13:38–39). But for everyone desiring to follow Jesus, He gives this threefold command.

1. We must *deny* ourselves. The Christian life is a selfless life. I believe there are two very practical results of denying ourselves. First, we are not to love the world or the things in the world (1 John 2:15–17). This does not mean that we cannot enjoy our lives. God created this world and placed us in it. After creation, God declared everything as "good" (Genesis 1:31). Enjoying God's creation is one of the most fulfilling things that we can experience. "Loving the world" means taking on the *philosophy* of the world, namely that this life is all that there is and therefore we should allow our own desires to drive our course. Scripture tells us that

love for the world indicates that the love of God is *not* in us (1 John 2:15) and by living this way we make ourselves enemies of God (James 4:4).

The other aspect of denying ourselves comes in placing the interests of others above our own (Philippians 2:3–4). This goes against everything in our fleshly nature. The world teaches us that we are to look out after our own interests but Jesus calls us to deny ourselves and take up the cause of those around us. Christians should be the most gracious, loving, and merciful people on the planet. When we treat others the way that we want them to treat us, we fulfill the Law of God (Matthew 7:12) and display a life of self-denial.

2.   We must *take up our cross*. For the first century hearer living in the Roman Empire, taking up a cross was a physical reality. Christians in that century would often suffer martyrdom for the name of Jesus. For us today, this is figurative language. The cross represents the ultimate in suffering and persecution. Practically speaking, taking up our cross means that we as believers should expect persecution. Jesus made this abundantly clear. If the world hated Him, they will in turn despise His followers (John 15:18–21). We are reminded that we are blessed when we experience persecution for the name of Jesus because it validates our place in His kingdom (Matthew 5:10–12). When we confess Jesus on earth, He will confess us in heaven (1 John 4:15, Matthew 10:32).

3.   We must *follow* Jesus. He designed us with a purpose, but we will only discover this life when we yield our plans to Him. Christians should always be sensitive to the leading and guiding of the Holy Spirit. This can only come when we decide to commit our ways to Him. I believe the issue of following Jesus comes down to how much we actually *trust* Him. Living by faith means knowing that God has our best interest in mind and that we can trust Him to

accomplish in us what only He can do. Following Jesus means that we need to be "all in."

There is a spiritual principle at work in this passage. The first half of the principle is the negative reality: "Whoever wishes to save his life will lose it." When we trade spiritual life for material things, we make one of the worst trades known to mankind. Material things are temporal, meaning that they are only tangible to this life and do absolutely nothing for us in eternity.

The other half of the principle is equally true: "Whoever loses his life for the sake of Christ will find it." Interestingly enough, "losing everything" for the sake of Christ actually works in our favor. We find abundant life here *and* in eternity. Just like the threefold command Jesus gives to His followers, this principle runs counter to anything the world understands.

We will close with two rhetorical questions Jesus uses to bring home this point. "For what does it profit a man if he gains the whole world and forfeits his own soul?" What a great question. The obvious answer is that he profits *nothing*. "Or what will a man give in exchange for his soul?" Again, the answer is obvious. He can offer *nothing* for his soul. We cannot buy eternal life. Simply put, to focus on material possessions is to invest in something that we cannot keep. Investing in God's kingdom is the most rewarding life and produces riches that last forever. How are you investing your life?

Mustard Seed Faith

Then the disciples came to Jesus privately and said, "Why could we not drive it out?" And He said to them, "Because of the littleness of your faith; for truly I say to you, *if you have faith the size of a mustard seed,* you will say to this mountain, 'Move from here to there,' and it will move; and nothing will be impossible to you. (Matthew 17:19–20)

Today: Read Matthew 17

The scene is a desperate one. A father who dearly loves his son falls at the feet of Jesus and begs for mercy. The father describes his son as a *lunatic.* The boy was being be hurled into fire and water. Scripture leaves no room for us to wonder what is causing these catastrophic events. It is a demon. The demonic are always after one thing: *destruction.* The attempt was to severely burn the boy or possibly drown him. What a horrible, hateful adversary we have. Although Jesus would cast this demonic force out of the boy, His indictment on the people is quite severe, "You unbelieving and perverted generation" (Matthew 17:17). The word "unbelieving" is the opposite of having faith in God, while the term "perverted" means to distort or turn aside from what should be. Despite these strong words, do not miss the beauty of this situation. The boy got to go home with his father, clear-minded and free! Satan traffics in unbelief, doubt, desperation, and fear. The tactics he uses are perverted at their core.

Later the disciples would have a moment to "debrief" the situation with Christ. The disciples' question is a good one, "Why couldn't we drive out the demon?" Jesus's answer was very direct, "Because of the *littleness* of your faith." As with all spiritual warfare, faith is essential. We are reminded that our faith acts as a spiritual shield and when our adversary fires his fiery arrows of doubt and despair into our lives, our faith is able to extinguish *all* of them (Ephesians 6:16). In other words, faith renders his efforts ineffective. So how much faith is required for such an outcome? Jesus describes the amount of faith required to that of a *mustard seed*. The meaning is obvious. The mustard seed is an incredibly small seed therefore if our faith can even rise to that level we will see God do mighty things in our lives. In this instance, it appears the disciples fell short of this kind of faith. How does Jesus describe the effect of mustard seed faith? This kind of faith is "mountain moving faith." It is faith that releases the power of God to act on our behalf. Jesus says that with this faith, "*nothing* will be impossible for us." Let me offer up three outcomes of a life lacking faith.

1. A lack of faith places limitations on seeing God's activity in our lives. Scripture teaches us that as Jesus moved about His hometown of Nazareth, He did not do many miracles *because* of their unbelief (Matthew 13:58). All throughout the gospels, we see Jesus responding *to* faith as He healed and delivered people from their infirmities. The Bible also tells us that the one who doubts (the opposite of faith) should not expect to receive anything from God (James 1:7).
2. A lack of faith puts limits on us. The power of God was available for healing this boy but the "littleness" of the disciples' faith hindered their ability to help.
3. A lack of faith does not produce results. Although Jesus had given the disciples the mission of performing healings, they were helpless to assist this desperate father.

Contrast that with mustard seed faith. Faith-filled living is God's design for us as believers and it glorifies Him in a number of ways.

1. Faith acknowledges the *power* of God.
2. Faith acknowledges the *goodness* of God.
3. Faith acknowledges the *authority* of God.
4. Faith affirms our trust in and *loyalty* to God.
5. Faith leads to *action*.

To have faith is to trust God. It means that we are willing to completely surrender ourselves *to* Him and to totally rely *on* Him. For this father, running to Jesus was the only option. It should be ours as well. Whatever you struggle with today, know that as a Christian, you have the ability to move mountains and it only takes faith the size of a mustard seed!

Not the Will of the Father

> What do you think? If any man has a hundred sheep, and one of them has gone astray, does he not leave the ninety-nine on the mountains and go and search for the one that is straying? If it turns out that he finds it, truly I say to you, he rejoices over it more than over the ninety-nine which have not gone astray. *So it is not the will of your Father who is in heaven that one of these little ones perish.* (Matthew 18:12–14)

Today: Read Matthew 18

Does God care about me? It's a question that we all ask at one time or another.

This question especially surfaces when we are going through incredibly difficult times.

In this passage, Jesus explains the importance of going after those who have gone astray. He equates this to a man who has one hundred sheep. If one of the sheep goes off from the herd, the sheep owner will instinctively go after the one that is lost. It is simply not enough for him to say, "Well, I still have ninety-nine others, I can afford to lose one." The question Jesus poses is a good one. "Does he not leave the ninety-nine on the mountains and go and search for the one that is straying?" The answer of course is, yes, he would obviously do that. Why? He goes after the lost animal because every one of the sheep is important. The sheep owner does not *have* to go after the sheep. He is not *obligated* in any way to rescue the sheep. He does so because every one of the sheep is important. Mankind is like the sheep. We have all gone astray. Jesus sees value in *every* human life, even those committed to rebelling against Him. He loves us in spite of ourselves and is dedicated to the proposition of saving those who will trust Him by faith. And heaven shares this affinity for rescuing mankind.

> "I tell you that in the same way, there will be *more joy* in heaven over one sinner who repents than over ninety-nine righteous persons who need no repentance" (Luke 15:7).

Jesus spoke these words after telling the parable of the lost sheep. Jesus says that there will be *more* joy in heaven over one repentant sinner than over ninety-nine righteous persons who need no repentance. We visualize heaven as an eternal place of joy. But here, Jesus compares the *level* of joy in heaven as being based on the repentant actions of a wayward person. That is pretty incredible when you stop to think about it. Turning from sin and turning to God spiritually frees us, bringing God joy, and all of heaven rejoices with Him. He mentions this concept again a few verses later after telling the parable of the lost coin.

> "In the same way, I tell you, there is *joy* in the presence of the angels of God over one sinner who repents" (Luke 15:10).

Does it matter to God whether a person repents? These verses seem to indicate that heaven itself is in celebratory mode every time this happens. Jesus concludes with a remarkable statement, "So it is not the will of your Father who is in heaven that one of these little ones perish?" What little ones? If you go back to the beginning of this chapter you will find the disciples asking Jesus who is greatest in the kingdom of heaven. To answer this question, Jesus calls a little child to himself (Matthew 18:2). What Jesus is saying is that God does not wish for any of those precious lives to perish. Do people perish? Of course they do. But it is not the will of God that they perish. Little children grow into adults but God does not stop caring about us just because we reach a certain age. If He loves us as children, He still loves us into and through adulthood. A passage that has helped me understand the heart of God is found in the Old Testament. In this passage, God is pleading with His people. Like the sheep, they continued to go astray and He was calling them back as an earthly father would invite back a wayward child.

> But if the wicked man turns from all his sins which he has committed and observes all My statutes and practices justice and righteousness, he shall surely live; he shall not die. All his transgressions which he has committed will not be remembered against him; because of his righteousness which he has practiced, he will live. Do I have any pleasure in the death of the wicked," declares the Lord God, "rather than that he should turn from his ways and live? (Ezekiel 18:21–23)

God is calling for repentance on the part of the wicked man. He is stating that the man's decision whether to repent or not is the criteria for God's actions. Wickedness would lead to death and destruction but repentance would lead to forgiveness and life. Then God poses the question, "Do I have any pleasure in the death of the wicked?" It is rhetorical and the answer is obviously, "no." God gets no pleasure from seeing someone perish, even the wicked. He goes on to add:

> "For I have no pleasure in the death of anyone who dies," declares the Lord God. "Therefore, repent and live" (Ezekiel 18:32).

God takes no pleasure in the death of anyone who dies. In fact, God continues to remind the wicked to repent so that they can live. This is God's desire.

Now back to Jesus and the sheep. We all like sheep have gone astray. God loves us and does not desire that any life perish but that all would come to repentance, so He gave us Jesus. He paid for the sins of all who would come to Him by faith. When a person is saved, God is pleased, the individual is set free, and all of heaven rejoices! Do you see the heart of God? Does God care about me? The answer is yes! God loves you. Jesus died for you. And it is not the will of the Father that you should perish. Trust in Him today!

There's room at the cross for you,
There's room at the cross for you,
Though millions have come, there's still room for one,
Yes there's room at the cross for you.

—Ira F. Stanphill (1914–1993)

Rejecting Jesus

Jesus said to him, "If you wish to be complete, go and sell your possessions and give to the poor, and you will have treasure in heaven; and come, follow Me." But when the young man heard this statement, *he went away grieving*; for he was one who owned much property. (Matthew 19:21–22)

Today: Read Matthew 19

It is always a good thing to ask the right questions. I believe we often tend to "spin our wheels" in an attempt to understand things that, in reality, are not that important. We would do well to prioritize our spiritual lives by asking the right questions. That is exactly what the young man in our passage today is doing. And what was the question? "Teacher, what good thing shall I do that I may obtain eternal life?" Jesus begins by questioning the man's reference to Him as "good." Jesus identifies God alone as the only One that can make the claim of being *perfectly* good. He then references the Law as the means by which the man will find life. The man asks for clarification as to which Laws and Jesus responds by mentioning several but not all of them. It is important to note here that Jesus is not teaching a works-oriented salvation. To do so would nullify the cross and the gospel (Galatians 2:21, 3:22, 26). Jesus is answering this man according to the old covenant, which was in effect until the completion of the new.

At this point the man seems to have a high view of his keeping the commandments. Because Jesus did not call him out on this claim, neither will we. Let's give him the benefit of the doubt and say that he *had* indeed kept all of those commandments. The truth: he was still lacking and he knew it. It is at this point that religion gets a foothold in the lives of many and leaves them with a false sense of their own righteousness. There are many morally good people in the world and for some it is that virtuous living that is equated with salvation. Nothing could be further from the truth. While righteous living should be the goal of every individual, it has no saving power whatsoever. This is a hard truth for the spiritually prideful. The only way for the Law to save is if it is kept to the very letter. By transgressing God's Law just once, we become guilty of the whole thing (James 2:10).

The gospel of Mark reveals Jesus's attitude toward the man. "Looking at him, Jesus felt a *love* for him" (Mark 10:21). So Jesus responds to the man's concern regarding his shortcomings with a specific instruction, "go and sell your possessions." Again, it is important to note that Jesus is not setting a precedent for all born-again believers in all generations to follow to the letter. If that were the case, then the only authentic believers would be those who sell everything they have (I haven't seen that in my experience). Rather Jesus is going straight to the heart of the matter. This man's possessions had become so important to him that he was not willing to part with them even if it meant missing out on eternal life. And how do we know this? Look at his reaction to Jesus's instructions, "But when the young man heard this statement, *he went away grieving*; for he was one who owned much property." He *wanted* the answer, but he did not *like* the answer. Jesus was talking about sacrifice and selfless living, something the man was unwilling to do. Jesus uses this as a teaching moment for the disciples by declaring:

> "Truly I say to you, it is hard for a rich man to enter the kingdom of heaven. Again I say to you, it is easier for a camel to go through the eye of a needle, than for a rich man to enter the kingdom of God" (Matthew 19:23–24).

When I think of this rejection of Jesus's love, it saddens my heart. Then I remember that I have done the same thing time after time against my Savior. Selfish living and clinging to things that do not ultimately matter, I can relate to this man. But there is good news!

> When the disciples heard this, they were very astonished and said, "Then who can be saved?" And looking at them Jesus said to them, "With people this is impossible, but with God *all things are possible*" (Matthew 19:25–26).

If you feel that you cannot be saved because of your track record, you would be incorrect. If you believe that doing good things will bring about or even solidify your salvation, you are also incorrect. If salvation were based on our moral perfection, then no one would be saved. But the things that are impossible for us are possible with God. Although believers should make every effort to honor God with their lives, the reality is that none of us have or ever will perfectly accomplish such a task. We are in need of a Savior and His name is Jesus! The only way we will miss out on salvation is to reject Jesus' love for us as demonstrated through the gospel (John 3:18). Call on Him today, trusting Him with your future, and enjoy the freedom of *knowing* that you belong to God!

Spiritual Grumbling

When those hired first came, *they thought that they would receive more*; but each of them also received a denarius. When they received it, *they grumbled at the landowner*, saying, "These last men have worked only one hour, and you have made them equal to us who have borne the burden and the scorching heat of the day." (Matthew 20:10–12)

Today: Read Matthew 20

I would like to say that I have never had this attitude before, but I have. I would like to say that I have never seen this attitude demonstrated in the lives of other Christians, but again, I have. It is the attitude of anger, resentment, and bitterness over the kindness of God. But why do Christian people get *angry* over God's *goodness* and *love* toward others? Why does the church stand in judgment of the lost instead of reaching out with healing hands and voices? And why do Christians resent others, being envious of God's blessings toward those individuals? What does the Bible say about this attitude and how do we guard against developing it?

First, we need to take a biblical look at this attitude. Secondly, we can use scripture to restructure our thinking so that the love of Jesus can freely flow out of our lives, making us more effective in representing a loving God.

Today's passage is a parable about the impartiality of God. It deals with the anger that can arise as a result of claiming spiritual privilege. In this parable, there are workers in the field. The landowner has made a promise to pay everyone working in the field a wage. Some of the workers came in to work at the third hour, some the sixth hour, and some the ninth. There were also some workers that did not show up until the eleventh hour. At the end of the day, the workers are called in to receive their wage. Consider the following:

> When those hired about the eleventh hour came, each one received a denarius. When those hired first came, *they thought that they would receive more*; but each of them also received a denarius (Matthew 20:9–10).

Can you guess what's going to happen next? If you guessed that someone is going to get upset, you are exactly right. Consider the next passage:

> When they received it, *they grumbled at the landowner*, saying, "These last men have worked only one hour, and *you have made them equal to us* who have borne the burden and the scorching heat of the day" (Matthew 20:11–12).

All of the workers were given the same wage because that was the arrangement that the landowner had made with the workers. To illustrate this arrangement that God has made with mankind, consider the following passages:

> "For God did not send His Son into the world to condemn the world but that the world through Him might be saved. *Whoever believes* in Him *is not* condemned" (John 3:17–18a).

> "*Whoever calls* on the name of the Lord *will* be saved" (Romans 10:13)

Sirs, what must I do to be saved? They said, "*Believe* in the Lord Jesus, and you *will* be saved, you and your household" (Acts 16:30b–31).

"Nevertheless, knowing that a man is not justified by works of the Law but through *faith* in Christ Jesus, even we have *believed* in Christ Jesus, so that we may be justified by *faith* in Christ and not by works of the Law, since by works of the Law, no flesh will be justified" (Galatians 2:16)

The workers were *all* paid the same because they had *all* worked in the field. The amount of time spent in the field was irrelevant because God had arranged for the same wage to be paid to *all* of the workers. Jesus died for our sins and *everyone* who calls on His name will be saved. Likewise, *everyone* who believes (trusts) in Him will inherit eternal life. The workers grumbled because they felt more *entitled* than the others. Why? It is because they had spent more time working in the field. Consider their argument:

"These last men have worked only one hour, and you have made them *equal* to us who *have borne the burden*" (Matthew 20:12).

It is a real danger for those particularly in vocational ministry, to be deceived into believing that because others around them are not "bearing the burden" the way they are, that those individuals are either not saved or do not deserve the same wage as they. The above passages speak volumes against that line of thinking. Salvation is not and never has been about human performance as a believer. Salvation comes when we trust in Jesus. Consider the following:

"Now to the one who works, his wage is not credited as a favor, but as what is due. But to the one who does not work, but *believes* in Him who justifies the ungodly, his *faith* is credited as righteousness" (Romans 4:4–5)

The workers grumbled, but not rightly so. When Christians exhibit this attitude, they are at fault for placing their value above others. It is our *faith* that allows us to be declared righteous, not our works. So how do we guard against these attitudes? Keeping these three biblical truths always before us will go a long way in eliminating this misguided attitude.

1. Understand that *everyone* is *equally* in need of a Savior (James 2:10).
2. Understand that there is *no boasting* in righteousness because it has been *given* to us as a *gift* (Romans 3:27–28).
3. Understand that you are to value others *above* yourself, not the other way around (Philippians 2:3–4).

Applying these principles to our lives will help guard against spiritual arrogance. If the workers in the field, had valued the lives of their fellow workers above themselves, they would not have been so preoccupied with their own work nor become frustrated by the lack of work coming from the others. This self-centered attitude does not belong in the church; it never has and it never will. The challenge for each of us is to jettison this attitude from our life, leaving room to develop a more Christ-like approach in our treatment of others. Then and only then will the character and nature of God be more accurately displayed to a watching world.

Seeing Hurting People

Truly I say to you that the tax collectors and prostitutes will get into the kingdom of God before you. For John came to you in the way of righteousness and you *did not believe* him; but the tax collectors and prostitutes *did believe* him; and you, seeing this, did not even feel remorse afterward so as *to believe him.* (Matthew 21:31–32)

Today: Read Matthew 21

Today we have another situation in which Jesus is dealing with the religious leaders of His day. These religious leaders were challenging Jesus's authority for His actions. It is important for us to understand that these were the very men who had been entrusted with the duty of guiding people in their spiritual lives. If we had a need for counseling or spiritual guidance during that era, we would have gone to these men. They were the teachers and the authority on all things scriptural. Yet they had a major flaw—they valued statutes and laws over people. While attempting to doctrinally defend their view of God and His righteousness, the Creator of the universe came to earth, stood right in front of them, and they did not even recognize Him. In addition, their zeal for the Law prohibited them from seeing hurting people around them and responding appropriately. Just in case we might think that this is being overstated, here are just a few examples of the Pharisees' spiritual shortsightedness.

A broken woman sits at the feet of Jesus. As she cries, she washes the feet of Jesus with her hair. Christ would later identify her as a woman "whose sins were many." The Bible simply refers to her as an *immoral* woman. She draws two reactions, one from a religious leader and one from Jesus. The Pharisee saw a woman with which he was not willing to associate. His disdain for her is evident in his statement, "If this man were a prophet He would know who and *what sort of person this woman is* who is touching Him, that she is a sinner." What is this woman's story? How did she get to this point in her life? He did not care about the answers to those questions because, quite frankly, he did not care about her. Contrast that to Jesus pronouncement of salvation over her life, "Your faith has saved you, go in peace." So this woman was the recipient of two reactions: condemnation from one, salvation, forgiveness, and spiritual freedom from Jesus (Luke 7:36–50).

A blind man sits begging. He has been blind for his entire life. He has never seen the sky, the faces of his parents, or even himself. He lives in physical darkness—that is until Jesus arrives. Jesus heals the man of his blindness, astonishing the crowd around Him. However, the religious leaders did not celebrate with Him, quite the contrary. In an attempt to trap Jesus, they questioned the man. They wanted this recently healed individual to "give glory to God", yet in the same breath they were accusing Jesus of being "a sinner." The Pharisees accused the man of being a disciple of Jesus (which would indicate salvation) only to acknowledge their own allegiance to the Law by declaring themselves disciples of Moses (which, ironically, would indicate spiritual deadness). Apparently, they were so angry and frustrated over seeing this man's recent good fortune that they reviled him, accused him of being "born entirely in sin", and then throwing him out. So this blind man, now seeing, was the recipient of two reactions: condemnation from one group, healing and restoration from Jesus (John 9:1–34).

A woman caught in the very act of adultery stands before Jesus. She has been brought there by the ravenous Pharisees. They are ready to see "justice" served. Knowing that the Law demands stoning for such an offense, they are awaiting Jesus's response. Jesus, seeing straight into their hearts, deals with them by saying, "He who is without sin among you, let him be the first to throw a stone at her." One by one the crowd disperses, being very aware of their own unworthiness. With all of her accusers gone, the woman stands alone before Christ and he declares, "I do not condemn you, either. Go. From now on sin no more." So one adulterous woman is the recipient of two reactions: condemnation from the Pharisees, forgiveness and restoration from Jesus (John 8:1–11).

So why is it that the chief priests and the elders pushed back against Jesus while sinful, hurting people ran to Him? I believe the key is found in today's passage. Jesus said that tax collectors and prostitutes were going to enter the kingdom *before* these religious leaders. The reason? The tax collectors and prostitutes *believed* and the religious did not (verse 32). As believers, we all need to acknowledge that we are as spiritually poor as anyone else, including tax collectors (thieves) and prostitutes. We need to remember that *our* spiritual life comes by faith when we place our trust in Christ. In turn, we are able to see the hurting people around us and respond to them in a Christ-like way, not a religious one. Our goal for others should be redemption and restoration, not condemnation and condescension. Jesus is our advocate and understands us completely (Hebrews 4:15–16). As believers we should reflect the same attitude. Do you see hurting people in your life? What are *you* willing to do about it?

The Two Commandments

Teacher, which is the great commandment in the Law? And He said to him, *"You shall love the Lord your God with all your heart, and with all your soul, and with all your mind."* This is the great and foremost commandment. The second is like it, *'You shall love your neighbor as yourself.'* *On these two commandments depend the whole Law and the Prophets.* (Matthew 22:36–40)

Today: Read Matthew 22

It seems that the Pharisees were always trying to catch Jesus in His words. Today, we look at one such event in which the question posed to Jesus was merely for the purposes of trapping Him (Matthew 22:35). Nevertheless, the question is a good one, so let's take the opportunity to hear Jesus's answer. And what was the question? Which of the commandments is the most important? Can you imagine what possibilities they expected to hear? "Maybe Jesus will identify adultery as the biggest prohibition. Or perhaps He will say murder." Whatever Jesus' answer, the Pharisees were ready to pounce.

But Jesus did not fall for such scheming. He told the Pharisees that *all* of the Law and the Prophets *hang* on these two commandments: *Love* God with your entire being (heart, soul, and mind) and *love* others as yourself. The Law and the Prophets constitute the entirety of the Old Testament of the Bible. Just like hanging up a coat when entering a house, Jesus says that you can *hang* all of the Old Testament on these two commandments. We know that God is love

(1 John 4:8) and that the first fruit of God's Spirit is love (Galatians 5:22). It should come as no surprise that Jesus would consolidate all of the Law into two commands both involving *love*.

Throughout the new covenant, we are reminded that love is not a side issue rather it is to take center stage in the life of a believer. Jesus says that loving one another is the way that the world will be able to recognize us (John 13:34–35). Jesus describes "treating others the way we want to be treated" as summing up the Law and the Prophets (Matthew 7:12). Love *is* the fulfillment of the Law (Romans 13:10) and "treating our neighbors properly," is referred to as the royal law. When we are able to do that, scripture says, "we do well" (James 2:8).

So we have a strong scriptural trail affirming the second greatest commandment identified by Christ. I believe most people can assess whether or not they are loving other people, but what about loving God? Since Jesus establishes that as the greatest commandment, is there a way that we can know if we are truly loving God? I believe Psalm 37 can help. It describes four areas commonly present in the life of those who truly love God. Answering these questions can help us determine where we stand.

1.   Do we *trust* God above all other people or things? (verse 3).

The essence of faith means to trust. If we claim to be believers in Jesus Christ, we are by default indicating that we trust Him and Him alone. When we trust in God, we are blessed and we find spiritual strength (Jeremiah 17:7–8). Trusting God gives us direction in our lives (Proverbs 3:5–6) and is the means by which we are eternally saved (John 3:18). To love God is to trust Him!

2.   Do we *delight* in God? (verse 4)

As Christians, we can enjoy a relationship with our Creator. If our Christian life seems heavy and burdensome, then we are missing out. Believers should delight in knowing God. The Psalm attaches a promise for those who delight in the Lord: "He will give them the desires of their heart." To love God is to delight in Him!

3.   Do we *commit* our ways to God? (verse 5)

To commit our ways to God is to dedicate everything that we do to the furthering of His kingdom. It is to focus on accomplishing things that have an eternal impact. To commit our way to God is to ask Him to direct our paths so that we may make the most of the time we have. To love God is to commit our ways to Him!

4.   Do we *rest* in the Lord's provision? (verse 7)

Lastly, believers are to rest in God. This is living in complete contentment with who we are and what we have. This type of rest goes beyond the world's understanding by allowing believers to relax while the rest of the world seems to be running crazy. Jesus invites everyone who is tired and burdened to come to Him and He promises that He *will* give them rest (Matthew 11:28). To love God is to rest in Him!

In summary, do you trust, delight in, commit your way to, and rest in God? If the answers are all yes, then I believe you can say with a good conscience that you are fulfilling the first and greatest commandment of loving God with your all of your heart, soul, and mind. If trusting, delighting, committing, and resting are not descriptions of your current spiritual life, talk to someone you trust about this issue.

There is one more thing we need to say. These two commandments work in tandem. Without loving God, we are sure to fall short of loving others the way Christ does. Likewise, we cannot claim love for a God who we *cannot* see without loving the people we *can* see (1 John 4:20). Here's to living out our lives in obedience to these two commandments!

True Discipleship

"But the greatest among you shall be your servant. Whoever exalts himself shall be humbled; and whoever humbles himself shall be exalted" (Matthew 23:11–12).

Today: Read Matthew 23

As we travel down life's road, we are sure to make mistakes. Learning from these missteps is important if our desire is to not repeat them. However, even greater than learning from our own mistakes is learning from the mistakes of others. Jesus begins this chapter of Matthew by discussing the Pharisees, pointing out their flaws, and giving us some practical examples of what *not* to do. Our passage today is a reminder of what true discipleship looks like. But before exploring what true discipleship *is*, let's learn from the Pharisees' mistakes discovering what it is *not*.

First, the Pharisees did not live a life consistent with what they were teaching (verse 3). They were operating out of the "Do as I say, not as I do" playbook. The church is often criticized for being full of hypocrites. I believe it is important for us to define hypocrisy. Hypocrisy is not an *absence* of mistakes rather it is pretending that we *do not make any*. The word hypocrisy comes from a theatrical term meaning "to put on a mask." Hypocrisy is pretending to be someone we are not. When we make a mistake, we should own up to it. This is something that the Pharisees were unwilling to do therefore their lives were not consistent with what they were teaching.

Secondly, the Pharisees were laying heavy legal burdens on people (verse 4). Living in Christ means living in the freedom that comes from God. The yoke of Jesus is pleasurable and His burden is light (Matthew 11:30). Once freed, we should stand firm against any form of legalism that can so easily enslave us (Galatians 5:1). Long-faced religion can be an outward expression of the inward reality that heavy burdens have been placed on our shoulders. Pharisaical teaching is a sure joy stealer and for that reason Jesus identified it as a flaw.

Thirdly, the Pharisees' motivation for their spiritual work was to be seen by others (verse 5). Phylacteries and tassels were outward adornments indicating their devotion to scripture and to prayer. The problem was that these outward symbols were used to impress others. Contrast that with what Jesus teaches about fasting, prayer, and giving (Matthew 6:1–18). When we engage in spiritual activities, it should be done in private, as much as possible. Others do not need to know when we are fasting. Praying in a private place brings great reward as does giving in secret. God sees what we do and the reward comes from Him. The Pharisees were after the approval of others rather than God.

Lastly, the Pharisees loved being popular with the people (verses 6–7). They were often given special consideration because of their position. Special seating at banquets and friendly greetings in the marketplace were just some of the perks they enjoyed. Everyone loves to be treated respectfully and with honor but Jesus denounced this in the Pharisees because it was what drove them. Jesus used an example to explain this problem:

> But do not be called Rabbi; for One is your Teacher, and you are all brothers. Do not call anyone on earth your father; for One is your Father, He who is in heaven. Do not be called leaders; for One is your Leader, that is, Christ. (Matthew 23:8–10)

Jesus identifies God as our heavenly Father and Himself as our Teacher and Leader. The capitalization of the words Teacher, Father, and Leader is important. We use these words in describing people in our lives but what Jesus is denouncing is placing mere men in the positions reserved for God alone. Yes, we have leaders and teachers in the church, but these people should be viewed as what they are, fallen humanity. The Pharisees had elevated themselves to levels far beyond what mankind has been given.

So now we have some Pharisaical characteristics to avoid in our Christian life. Having acknowledged these flaws, we now need to define true discipleship. True discipleship involves leaving a lofty position to become the servant of everyone else. It is no wonder that the Christian life does not look attractive to the world. Believers are always looking for ways to diminish themselves in order to elevate others. This is exactly what Christ did. He left heaven and took on the flesh of man. He came to offer up Himself as the atoning sacrifice for our sin, once for all. He traded His rightful place as God for that of servant. I believe this is what He meant when He said:

> It is not this way among you, but whoever wishes to become great among you shall be your servant, and whoever wishes to be first among you shall be your slave; *just as the Son of Man did not come to be served, but to serve, and to give His life a ransom for many.* (Matthew 20:26–28)

The principle for this reality can be summed up in the statement, "Whoever exalts himself shall be humbled; and whoever humbles himself shall be exalted." True discipleship requires that we become less in order for Christ and others to become more. The Pharisees missed the point and made their spiritual service about themselves. True discipleship may go without human accolades, but God is watching and for anyone willing to take this selfless road less traveled, the rewards are eternal!

The Return of Jesus

Therefore be on the alert, for you do not know which day your Lord is coming. But be sure of this, that if the head of the house had known at what time of the night the thief was coming, he would have been on the alert and would not have allowed his house to be broken into. For this reason you also must be ready; *for the Son of Man is coming at an hour when you do not think He will.* (Matthew 24:42–44)

Today: Read Matthew 24

I have to admit that I have never had much of an obsession about the second coming of Jesus. I know that He will return someday but I believe all of us have things that we should be focusing our attention on today and each day that we live. With that being said, there does not seem to be a shortage of people who *do* focus on prophecy and the issues surrounding the end times. In our passage today, Jesus provides us with valuable information regarding His own return. The Bible can shine a light and give us clarity on a topic so often distorted and misrepresented.

"But of that day and hour no one knows, not even the angels of heaven, nor the Son, but the Father alone" (Matthew 24:36)

No one knows when this event will take place. Anyone who claims to have that privileged information is misinformed. Scripture instructs us that not even the angels nor Jesus know the hour. This information resides with God the Father alone. This truth should eliminate any, if not all, of the speculation that exists in our world today. Knowing that God knows the hour, frees the church up to focus on what has been entrusted to us, preaching the gospel to all creation.

> For the coming of the Son of Man will be just like the days of Noah. For as in those days before the flood they were eating and drinking, marrying and giving in marriage, until the day that Noah entered the ark, and they did not understand until the flood came and took them all away; so will the coming of the Son of Man be. (Matthew 24:37–39)

Jesus uses an illustration from history. The coming of Christ will be like the days of Noah. Eating, drinking, marrying, and giving in marriage are all phrases pointing out that the normal ebb and flow of life was taking place in those days. The people neither understood nor expected that a flood was to come and put an end to life as they knew it. Likewise, Jesus's return will also come as people are going about their normal routines.

> "Then there will be two men in the field; one will be taken and one will be left. Two women will be grinding at the mill; one will be taken and one will be left" (Matthew 24:40–41).

These verses reveal the spiritual reality that not everyone will be ready for Christ's return. One person being taken and one being left behind is a reference to the rapture of the church. Those who have been born again and belong to Jesus are those who are prepared. They are sons and daughters of God and heirs to His kingdom therefore the day will not catch them by surprise. Even though the specifics behind Jesus's return are hidden to all of us, the expectation of His return should be ever present in the heart of a believer. Those that are left are those who are not saved and have no place in the kingdom of God. Tragically, many people live out their entire existence on this earth without even a passing thought or care about what lies beyond this life. Upon Christ's return, not everyone will be ready. This is a reality we should all consider.

Jesus concludes with an admonition for us to be alert and ready for His coming. For the very reason that we do *not* know the timing, we should continue to run our race as we look forward to the day when all things will be made right. Rather than speculate on the timing, we should care enough about the spiritual well-being of our family members and neighbors that we are willing to do whatever is necessary to lead them to Jesus. This should be the mission of every believer.

Using Your Gifts

To one he gave five talents, to another, two, and to another, one, each according to his own ability; and he went on his journey. Immediately the one who had received the five talents went and traded with them and gained five more talents. In the same manner the one who had received the two talents gained two more. But he who received the one talent went away and dug a hole in the ground and hid his master's money. (Matthew 25:15–18)

Today: Read Matthew 25

This life matters. Each of us is specifically designed to accomplish what only we can do. When we consider the amount of time some people spend comparing themselves to others, we begin to realize the power of the enemy's influence in convincing people that they are inferior to others. The truth is that if we do not use the gifts given to us, the job we were designed to fulfill will either go undone or someone else will receive the blessing for being faithful to accomplish it. Every believer has been given a purpose to fulfill in this life. The Bible refers to these as *spiritual gifts*. Below are some considerations involving the use of these gifts.

1. Spiritual gifts are *from* God.

> "Now there are *varieties* of gifts, but the *same*
> Spirit. And there are *varieties* of ministries, and
> the *same* Lord" (1 Corinthians 12:4–5).

Notice that spiritual gifts come in a number of different varieties. Likewise, ministries come in all different shapes and sizes. But all of the gifts come from the *same* God. God's Spirit is our source of power to achieve God-sized results. When the gifting is being used to make an eternal impact in the lives of others, then we can know it is from God.

2. Not everyone has the *same* gift.

> "For just as we have many members in one body
> and *all the members do not have the same function*,
> so we, who are many, are one body in Christ,
> and individually members one of another"
> (Romans 12:4–5).

As Christians, we are all members of the same body (the church) but we do not all share the same function. God created each of us with a specific personality and has gifted each of us with a uniqueness that no one else can fulfill. Comparing ourselves to one another can rob us of discovering our own purpose and worth. We all have different functions and purposes to fulfill.

3. Spiritual gifts are to benefit *others*.

> And He gave some as apostles, and some as
> prophets, and some as evangelists, and some as
> pastors and teachers, for the *equipping* of the
> saints for the work of service, to the *building up*
> of the body of Christ. (Ephesians 4:11–12)

Our gifts are not only for ourselves. We are gifted to benefit others. Two functions of spiritual gifts, particularly for pastors and teachers, are to *equip* others to carry out their own purposes and to assist in *building up* the church. When Christians are equipped, they become stronger. The gifting of God is to create a church that is spiritually strong and prepared to make an impact in the world.

In today's passage, Jesus uses a parable to explain the kingdom of God. He compares it to three men who were given talents (gifts). In the parable, God gave one man five talents, while giving another two, and yet another just one. This illustrates our first two points. The gifts are *from* God but they *varied* depending on who was receiving them. The point of the parable is that only two of the men used their gifts, earning a return on God's investment. These "faithful servants" were declared such and received the following response from God:

> "Well done, good and faithful slave. You were
> faithful with a few things, I will put you in charge
> of many things, enter into the joy of your master"
> (Matthew 25:21–23).

The third man was afraid to use his talent and went and buried it in the ground. He was not declared faithful rather God referred to him as a "wicked and lazy" servant. What he was given was taken away and given to someone else.

This parable is a stark reminder of how important it is for believers to use their spiritual gifts. I believe the most fulfilling thing we can do in this life is to effectively operate in the spiritual gifting that God has designed for us. Your gifting is to be enjoyed. It should bring you fulfillment. When you discover and utilize your spiritual gift it will be confirmed by others around you. If you are unsure of your purpose, talk to those who know you best. There are a variety of gifts and we do not all have the same function but every believer has a role to play. Are you fulfilling your purpose?

Denying Jesus

"Then he began to curse and swear, 'I do not know the man!' And immediately a rooster crowed" (Matthew 26:74).

Today: Read Matthew 26

We know the story well. Peter, a self- proclaimed *loyal* follower, will bow to the human pressure of fear. It was easy to follow Jesus on those bright sunny days when everything was great. Jesus was teaching and the disciples were soaking it up. Healing and miraculous signs were so numerous one could not even count them. But now Jesus is gone, being held by government officials. He spoke a lot about this day and told them that they should not be surprised when these things happened. Yet it wasn't that long ago that Peter was pledging his allegiance to Jesus, a loyalty that Peter was willing to follow even to death. And now the time has come to test his devotion.

Approached by a servant girl and recognizing Peter as a follower of Jesus, she points him out. He denies knowing anything of what she speaks. Another servant girl approaches with the same observation, but still denial. As the bystanders began to gather, they too questioned Peter regarding his status of being a Jesus follower. This time, with curses from his mouth, Peter denies it all. The rooster crows—well you know the rest.

Before we start Peter-bashing, let's be honest. Haven't we all been there at one time or another? A missed opportunity to share Jesus, a camouflaging of our faith so that we could land the new job, or just not wanting to be thought of as "weird." All of these are more common than we might think. And what is the driving force behind these denials? I believe it can be primarily attributed to *fear*. Peter thought he was ready to commit unto death, but when it came right down to it, he wasn't. It is fear that usually keeps us from stepping out of our comfort zone to share Jesus. Fear of losing our job can cause us to hide our faith at work. And it is fear stemming from social pressure that causes multitudes of believers to choose the path of least resistance when it comes to their Christian life. I would like to offer up two reminders of what our life in Christ is to be.

> "Therefore everyone who confesses Me before men, I will confess him before My Father who is in heaven. But whoever denies Me before men, I will also deny him before My Father who is heaven" (Matthew 10:32–33).

You can look at that passage in a negative, fearful light and many people do. But look at the tremendous *promise* we have from Jesus for those of us that outwardly profess the name of Christ. Every time that we are faithful to stand and take on the darkness of this world, we should remind ourselves of the day when we will stand before God and Jesus will smile and declare us as those who belong. Secondly, there is the issue of being the light of the world.

> You are the light of the world. A city set on a hill cannot be hidden, nor does anyone light a lamp and put it under a basket, but on the lampstand, and it gives light to all who are in the house. Let your light shine before men in such a way that they may see your good works and glorify your Father who is in heaven. (Matthew 5:14–16)

I do not believe it is helpful to live our lives continually announcing the darkness that is in the world. If we were in an unfamiliar room, completely in the dark, what would announcing the darkness do for helping us navigate the space? Rather, if we had the smallest of lights, we could dispel the darkness in a moment by shining that light, no matter how small (that reminds me of mustard seed faith). Darkness cannot stand in the face of light. Confessing Jesus and holding up the simplicity of the gospel will always yield results. Yes, some will run from the light for fear that they will be exposed (John 3:20) but others will be healed because of our faithfulness. So turn that light on, even in the midst of what seems to be overwhelming darkness—it's not!

Let's close with Peter. Yes, he denied Jesus three times. But Jesus reinstated him with a series of three questions (I think that is significant). I believe this goes way beyond forgiveness on the part of Christ. Jesus was giving Peter the opportunity to heal from his denials and three failed attempts would require three victories (John 21:15–17). If you have struggled with being faithful in your walk with Christ, take heart! Just like in the life of Peter, Jesus forgives failures and is ready to hand you some victories! He is ready and willing, are you?

A Game Changer

"And Jesus cried out again with a loud voice and yielded up His spirit. And behold, the veil of the temple was torn in two from top to bottom, and the earth shook and the rocks were split" (Matthew 27:50–51).

Today: Read Matthew 27

The crucifixion of Jesus and subsequently His burial and resurrection are the central themes in which all of human existence revolves. This unequalled, monumental action on the part of God changed forever the way He deals with mankind. While God remains unchanging, His gift of offering Jesus as the propitiation for the sins of the world allows Him to exercise His mercy and grace on believers while retaining all of His just and righteous nature. Even when rejected by mankind, this one act of God's love is a game changer for those who trust in Jesus. There are no less than three major ways that the crucifixion transforms the spiritual reality of born-again believers.

1. Believers are now justified before God completely *apart* from works.

   But now *apart* from the Law the righteousness of God has been manifested, being witnessed by the Law and the Prophets, even the righteousness of God *through faith* in Jesus Christ for *all those who believe*; for there is no distinction... for we

> maintain that a man is *justified by faith apart from works* of the Law. (Romans 3:21–22,28)

Everyone who belongs to Jesus has had their sins forgiven once and for all based on *His* righteous action on the cross (Romans 5:18–19). We have a spiritual enemy that would like to convince us otherwise by keeping us locked up by our transgressions of the past. Any opportunity he has to accuse us or remind us of moral failures he gladly takes knowing that this mindset will prohibit us from enjoying and walking in the victory already bought for us on the cross. Believers should no longer assess their spiritual lives on their *own* performance rather we should trust in Jesus's obedience on the cross as the basis for *His* righteousness applied *to* us by faith (Romans 4:4–5). The cross allows us to declare to the world that, "Mankind is justified by faith *apart* from works of the Law."

2. Jesus has established a *new* covenant for those who believe.

> But now He (Jesus) has obtained a *more excellent* ministry, by as much as He (Jesus) is also the mediator of a *better* covenant, which has been enacted on *better* promises. For if that first covenant had been faultless, there would have been no occasion sought for a second. When He said, "A new covenant," He has made the first obsolete. But whatever is becoming obsolete and growing old is ready to disappear. (Hebrews 8:6–7,13)

Through the cross, God has established a new covenant with mankind. It is worth noting that the old covenant (the ten commandments) was established between God and the people of Israel. The Gentile nations (the rest of the world) were not included in this covenant. For someone to impose the old covenant on the church today is to ignore the better covenant establish by Jesus on the cross and also places burdens on believers that were never intended for us to bear. Our spiritual enemy would like to convince us that the old covenant, with its legal requirements, is still somehow in effect, but the old covenant is now obsolete. The cross allows us to enjoy favor *from* God and to have a relationship *with* God by faith.

3. Believers now have *direct* access to God without the assistance of the clergy.

> Therefore, since we have a great high priest who has passed through the heavens, Jesus the Son of God, let us hold fast our confession. For we do not have a high priest who cannot sympathize with our weaknesses, but One who has been tempted in all things as we are, yet without sin. Therefore let us draw near with *confidence* to the throne of grace, so that we may receive mercy and find grace to help in time of need. (Hebrews 4:14–16)

The cross gives us direct access to God. The curtain in the temple separated the most holy place from the rest of the temple. This room was not accessible to everyone rather was reserved for the high priest and even he could enter only once a year. When Jesus gave up His spirit, the curtain was torn from top to bottom symbolizing the spiritual reality that *all* can come to the throne of God by faith. Christians can confidently approach God at any time because of the establishment of the new covenant. Our high priest is now Christ Himself and *He* acts as our mediator (1 Timothy 2:5). Jesus understands us and can sympathize with us because He has walked in our shoes, yet without sin. Our spiritual enemy would like to convince us that God gets angry when we make mistakes and would like to see us flee from God and His love instead of confidently approaching Him and receiving grace and mercy to assist us in time of need. The cross allows us to know that we are accepted by God.

Belonging to Jesus yet living as if we have to earn our salvation is to miss out on spiritual freedom. Belonging to Jesus and yet living as if the old covenant is still in effect is failure to acknowledge that

He has fulfilled the Law. Belonging to Jesus yet failing to approach Him with confidence is to overlook our right as children of God. If you are a Christian, rejoice! The cross has forever changed your spiritual reality! My challenge is to begin living out that reality today!

Finally, in light of these spiritual "game changers," it is possible for someone to miss out on this spiritual truth. To reject Jesus is to reject His salvation. In reality, a non-believer has the opposite spiritual situation. Apart from Christ our sins are *not* forgiven. Apart from Christ we are still under the Law. Apart from Christ we cannot approach God with confidence. But here is the good news. We can call on the name of the Lord and receive salvation (Romans 10:13). We can be transformed from lost to found, from spiritually blind to one who now has sight. If you have never prayed and asked God to save you, then the cross remains ineffective in your life. Why would you not do that right now? I encourage you to do so.

Our Mission

> And Jesus came up and spoke to them, saying, "*All authority* has been given to Me in heaven and on earth. *Go* therefore and make disciples of all the nations, *baptizing* them in the name of the Father and the Son and the Holy Spirit, *teaching* them to observe all that I commanded you; and lo, I am with you always, even to the end of the age." (Matthew 28:18–20)

Today: Read Matthew 28

I believe the church today should adopt a renewed focus on the mission that Jesus has left us prior to His ascension from the earth. Jesus has been given *all* authority in heaven and on earth and He informed the disciples that He *would* equip them to carry out their mission of making disciples. Consider the following:

> "But you will *receive power* when the Holy Spirit has come upon you; and you shall be My witnesses both in Jerusalem, and in all Judea and Samaria, and even to the remotest part of the earth" (Acts 1:8).

So with Jesus as our authority and with the Holy Spirit as our source of supply, let's fulfill our threefold mission.

1. We are to *go* into the world and preach the gospel to all nations (Mark 16:15). This verse can be translated "as we go" because there is an assumption of action already taking place. All of us are "going" throughout our daily routine. As we go, we are to look for opportunities to share the good news with others. Relying on the Holy Spirit for the opportunity, the words, and the timing is essential in discovering "divine appointments" in our lives.

2. We are to *baptize* those who receive Christ. Baptism is an outward expression of an inward, spiritual reality. When we are born again, our first response should be to publicly affirm what has taken place in our lives. It is the church's responsibility to guide new believers in baptism, celebrating their spiritual restoration with them. Baptism is to be done in the name of the Father, and the Son, and the Holy Spirit.

3. We are to *teach* believers so that spiritual growth can take place. Teaching is an important part of the spiritual maturation process. It is possible for new believers to receive salvation only to fail to grow spiritually in their faith. Christians who neglect the study of God's Word will inevitably find themselves being tossed around by every teaching that is in the world (Ephesians 4:14). Spiritual growth is essential for us to experience the abundant life that Jesus desires for us to receive (John 10:10).

When the church focuses on its primary mission of preaching the gospel and making disciples, the world begins to change, one heart at a time. I believe that placing Christ as priority one is ultimately the only way in which society will begin to see healing and restoration.

If you have been reading through the gospel of Matthew, let me congratulate you on completing your journey! Keep in mind that this gospel begins with a genealogy of Christ and ends with the commission to go and make disciples. Let's make this mission our priority!

Section 2: Reading Through the Gospel of Matthew

Epilogue

I sincerely hope that this study has brought you much joy and excitement! I would like to encourage you to continue growing in your knowledge *of* and walk *with* Jesus Christ. If you have been studying with a group, consider keeping the group together and begin a new study. I hope that you find yourself spiritually stronger than when you began. May God richly bless you as you continue to give Him first priority in your life!

> Come to Me, all who are weary and heavy-laden, and I will give you rest. Take My yoke upon you and learn from Me, for I am gentle and humble in heart, and *you will find rest for your souls*. For My yoke is easy and My burden is light. (Matthew 11:28–30)

Coming Soon: *mytwocents* Volume 2!

About the Author

Dr. Steve Edge is a retired public educator from the state of Texas. He has pastored two churches and holds a master's degree in Christian education and a doctorate in educational ministry. Steve and his wife, Diane, are native Texans but love to spend time in the Colorado mountains as often as they can. It is their sincere desire that this book will assist you in your walk with Christ.

CPSIA information can be obtained
at www.ICGtesting.com
Printed in the USA
BVHW082226080221
599628BV00001B/183